40 YEARS OF LOVING AND JOYFUL MARRIAGE. HOW TO GET THERE?

Romans 12:10 "*Be devoted to one another in love. Honor one another above yourselves.*"

Gary Cunitz

Library of Congress Cataloging–in–Publication Data

Cunitz, Gary 2023

40 Years of Loving and Joyful Marriage. How To Get There? / Gary Cunitz

p. cm.

ISBN: 978-1-961392-69-4

1. Christianity relationships –marriages – spouses – dating – self-improvement

2. Christian marriages – growth – understanding

3. Christian aspects – beliefs – growth – spiritual

John 3:16

"For God so loved the world, that he gave his one and only Son, that whoever believes in him should not perish but have eternal life."

Dedication

I dedicate this book to my family and thank them for all the love and support they have given me. Without them I would have been lost in the wilderness.

My special and loving dedication goes to my wife, Claudette. You are the rock and stability of our family. Your love and dedication to the truth is an example for all of us on how we should live our Christian lives.

Acknowledgment

I, Gary Cunitz, acknowledge the Lord Jesus Christ and His glory and love towards all mankind.

Romans 10:9 *"that if you confess with your mouth Jesus is Lord and believe in your heart that God raised Him from the dead, you will be saved."*

If God is before us, who dare be against us!

Table Of Contents

About the Author

Hi I'm Gary Cunitz,

God has blessed me with the most amazing wife, family, children, and experiences I could have ever imagined. Coming from a middle class family in Southern California I never dreamed what God's plan was for my future. I assumed that the rest of my life was going to be playing volleyball on the beach and surfing till I was 80 years old.

All the events in my past life lead me to where I am now. God placed me in a Christian University (Pepperdine) where I found Jesus. One blessing lead to another blessing and all of sudden I found myself in a real estate class meeting my future wife. And so my life began.

I wrote this book so I could share with others that marriage can be joyous and rewarding. Biblical scripture tells us and guides us through times of trouble in a marriage and as single individual. I pray the biblical references in this book and also my relationship to these scriptures will shed light and meaning to achieve a joyous and loving marriage for you.

The Bible says that you should share your good fortune. I pray that my good fortune and experiences can be a blessing to you.

God Bless You,

Gary Cunitz

Introduction

"Do as I say and not as I do."

As a person who has experienced the joys and challenges of a 40-year marriage, I understand the need for guidance in matters of the heart and marital relationship. Growing up, I wished for a book that would help me navigate the complexities of finding the right partner, building a strong relationship, and raising a family.

That's why I wrote this book, to help others avoid the pitfalls I encountered and to provide practical, down-to-earth advice for creating a fulfilling and lasting marriage.

I begin by exploring the initial stages of attraction, courtship, and romance, emphasizing the importance of understanding oneself before seeking a partner. Throughout the book, I draw on biblical teachings to provide insight and guidance on key issues in life and marriage.

<u>Psalm 143:10</u> *"Teach me to do your will, for you are my God; may your good spirit lead me on level ground."*

Effective communication is crucial to a successful marriage, yet it is often one of the most challenging aspects to master. I share my own experiences and those of other couples to highlight common communication pitfalls and offer practical solutions for improving communication skills.

While I am not a marriage counselor or psychologist, my faith in God has provided me with insight and wisdom that I believe will be helpful to others. I hope this book will encourage and support couples in their marriages and help individuals grow in their relationship with Jesus Christ.

I also encourage readers to seek additional support and resources from Christian organizations offering marriage counseling and support. Together, may we continue to walk with Jesus and experience the joy and love that comes from a strong, Christ-centered marriage. For the kingdom and glory will always be his, forever, through Jesus Christ, we pray.

Amen!

My Letter to You

Dear Christian Brothers and Sisters,

Thank you for choosing '40 Years of Loving and Joyful Marriage. How To Get There?' I pray that the Lord Jesus Christ blesses you, your family, and your marriage as he has blessed mine.

This book is a personal, heartfelt guide for single, engaged, newly married Christians and those who have been married for a long time. I've compiled my personal memoirs, notes, and experiences to help Christians in their quest to make relationships and marriages succeed with joy and love through Jesus Christ's teachings.

God has blessed me with the most amazing wife, family, children, and experiences I could have never imagined. I would like to share my experiences with Biblical references that will help draw a correlation between life's experiences and God's divine teaching.

The Bible offers solutions for marriages to be strengthened and also for those individuals that are seeking relationships and not sure what marriage is all about.

These timeless Biblical principles explore the foundation that makes a marriage strong in knowing and identifying marriage partners, strengthening a marriage, communication, trust, companionship, connection, commitment, compromise, family balance, and love.

I've also included in my book '40 Years of Loving and Joyful Marriage. How To Get There?' daily scripture relating to and addressesing life's issues with your Christian partner, yourself, and your family.

I'll describe this book as a Christian self-help book that provides healing and scriptural messages for singles and marriages.

For Christians to survive, especially Christian families, we need to return to God's blessings and teachings. When God is at the center of marriage (and an individual), we experience peace and love that forms the foundation on which marriages are built.

Once again, thank you for choosing my book, and may God bless you and your family.

Sincerely, Gary Cunitz.

Chapter 1: The Beginning

<u>Ephesians 4:32</u>: *"Be kind and compassionate to one another, forgiving each other, just as in Christ God forgave you."*

Be patient in finding the right companion

Marriage is not easy; it takes compromise, understanding, respect, forgiveness, and commitment. This book is dedicated to helping Christian marriages have a long, lasting, and fulfilled marriage enshrouded with joy and love.

Let's start at the beginning... You are single, carefree, and have few responsibilities. Your only commitment may be to call your parents once a week, if that. Life was simple and fun, but you felt a small nudge that something was missing.

What could that something be? Growing up, I was always athletic. I never had time to think about dating or even talking to girls. All types of sports preoccupied my time. If I was not playing sports, I was watching sports on television. My typical day involved meeting with neighborhood kids after school to play baseball in our cul-de-sac or basketball in one of the driveways.

The opposite sex was always a sister of a teammate or an opponent, and I was too busy competing with the opposing player and striving to improve in the sport I was playing.

At a young age, I learned that practice was the only way to get better and avoid losing, so girls were a nuisance to my focus on improvement. It wasn't until I turned eighteen that I became interested in dating girls and deviated from my sports routine.

My first real date was during my senior year in high school. On my first dates, I recall talking about sports the entire time. Looking back, I must have been boring as anything.

Are you devoted to a hobby or a sport? Are you an individual that is happy with yourself? There is strength in the inner confidence. I have always been happy and enjoyed my own company.

You may call it self-confidence or inner peace, but whatever you call it, self-happiness is a strength everyone can attain. We are created in the image of God, which means our Heavenly Father has not only bestowed us with external physical appearances but also inner spirit of peace, and joy with a destiny.

Gods Control:

I believe in my soul that my inner peace helped me to be able to identify the character and spirit of my future soul mate.

1.1 Dating is key to identifying compatibility

How many dates have you been on and knew right away that this was not the one? They may be too egotistical, loud, have compromising habits, or have a different moral compass. These differences can make it challenging to envision a future together.

However, you cannot overlook what God has placed in your life. Everyone that is in our life has a great quality; some have greater qualities than others. When dating or hanging with friends, take note of these qualities. When I met my wife, she had the sum of qualities from other relationships that set her head and shoulders above anyone else. She was the most perfect person I had ever met, and my job was to convince her that I was the perfect match for her. It is important to note that no one is perfect, and we all have flaws. But when you come across someone with the qualities you are looking for, that is a special person for you.

It's important to remember that understanding human qualities requires experience, time, and prayer. We should remain humble and patient while seeking that perfect match, remembering that God has us in the palm of His hand. Believing in God can provide reassurance during this process, and the book of Matthew can serve as a source of comfort.

Mathew 7:7: *"Ask, and it will be given to you, seek, and you will find, knock, and it will be opened to you."*

Your high school sweetheart, whom you believe to be the only person you will ever love, may not end up being your life partner. Of course, there are rare exceptions, but trust me, explore and play the field. I'm not speaking of being a Playboy or Playgirl, but I am saying have friends, lots of friends. Some of these friends may turn into a relationship. You have heard the cliché, "if it's meant to be,"… let time be your friend. (Sorry for the pun, I could not resist).

"Friends make the best life partners..." What a wise and in-depth idea. Whoever said that should be awarded the Nobel Peace Prize. Imagine your whole life with your best friend.

1.2 Courtship

Courtship plays a crucial role in understanding your future partner, allowing you to get to know them better and determine whether or not you are compatible with them in the long run.

When it comes to dating, it's natural to want to put your best foot forward. From opening car doors to being an attentive listener, the early stages of a relationship are all about making a good first impression.

We know that first impressions can be crucial, so we tend to adjust our behavior to impress the other person. However, this desire to impress can sometimes lead to boasting or bragging, which is best avoided. We all want to impress others intentionally or subconsciously.

We want to be seen as exciting, smart, successful, athletic, caring, and compassionate. We want the other person to want to go out with us again and again and again.

The beginning of a relationship is the foundation of a healthy, strong friendship and possible marriage.

How do you know what you are looking for? It starts with knowing yourself. Who are you? You can't identify the future companion if you do not know yourself. The Psalms said it best:

Psalms 139:13: *"For you created my inmost being; you knit me together in my mother's womb."*

Who are they, and who are you?

God created you to be special, not like your neighbor or that famous athlete. Get to know who you are. Do not compare yourself to others. You are unique and have qualities that others do not have. You are a masterpiece that God has created.

Let's start with what you like. What do you like to do? Know yourself before you try to understand others. I feel that most successful relationships start with couples that have something in common. This is especially true for long and lasting marriages. The rule that needs to be followed is that couples should always have something in common!

It's true that over time, a person's true character and moral standards will reveal themselves, and you may discover their flaws such as being a poor listener, extremely messy, or not as successful as you thought. In the worst-case scenario, you may find out they don't like kittens or puppies, which could be a deal-breaker. You have wasted 6 months, maybe even several years, with that person,

4

and they turn out to be the complete opposite you had hoped, even longed for… How do you cut through the weeds from the start and have an understanding of what the other person is all about?

1.3 Dating and Understanding the other side

First of all, how did you meet? Was it at a bar? Was it in school? Was it through the Internet? Or maybe it was a set-up from one of your friends. If you met in a bar, the success rate has a very low percentage of a couple surviving. You need to be honest with yourself and ask, does this person congregate in bars?

1.4 Where to find your perfect match

Do they look forward to the end of the day when they can go and hang out in the nightclub? What is their attraction to the nightlife? I found that most barflies are very shallow in character. Not all but most! One thing that 'Bar Dwellers' do very well is small talk. However, small talk is not enough to build a long-lasting relationship. You need to ask yourself if you want to spend your life in a bar or if nightlife is your end game. If you enjoy the bar scene and the other person does, too, then it may be a perfect match.

However, meeting someone in a bar doesn't always lead to a disastrous outcome. It's possible to meet someone who shares your interests and values. One of my best friends met his wife in a bar, and they have been happily married for over 30 years. Don't get me wrong; this is not a judging issue! This is a reality check to open your eyes, understand human circumstances, and ask yourself the right questions.

By asking the hard questions, be ready to act on the uncomfortable answers. Be honest with yourself; you will be so much happier in the end. Meeting someone in school is probably the most revealing of who that person is.

Meeting their friends, for example, can reveal a lot about the person as individuals tend to associate with those who share similar values and interests. By observing how they treat each other, one can determine whether they value respect, punctuality, consideration for others' feelings, and possess a strong moral compass. You can also learn a lot about someone by observing how they spend their free time. Are they motivated and driven, or do they tend to lie around? Do they have a good work ethic, demonstrated by diligence in completing homework and assignments and perhaps attending religious services? Do they have a good work-life balance, or are they constantly stressed and overburdened? Are they tidy and organized, or messy and disorganized?

All of these factors can help you get a better understanding of someone's personality, values, and lifestyle. By paying attention to these details, you can make more informed decisions about who you want to spend your time with and build relationships with.

Another great place to meet that special someone is what I call the common ground acquaintance. This is my favorite place that I would direct everyone to explore. This approach involves exploring your interests and hobbies to find groups or clubs that align with your passions. For example, if you enjoy cooking, consider joining a cooking class, or if you're a wine enthusiast, a wine club might be a great fit. If you're athletic, there are numerous clubs available through parks and rec departments, health clubs, and community leagues that cater to a wide range of interests, from softball and bowling to mountain climbing, martial arts, golf, and more.

Similarly, if you have a talent for creating art or crafts, consider exploring local pottery, woodworking, or photography groups. Alternatively, if you enjoy reading or volunteering for charities, church functions can be an excellent place to meet like-minded people.

Meeting someone in a club, organization, or church means you will have something in common immediately, making it easier to strike up a conversation. Half of the unknown is already figured out when you have immediately identified something in common.

Dating sites are another modern-day solution to finding a partner. However, there are inherent risks involved, such as romance scammers. In 2020, the FBI reported over $350 million in losses from romance scams, which increased by 50% from 2019. Scammers can be manipulative and tug at heartstrings, leading to financial loss and emotional pain. It is essential to be cautious when meeting internet connections because falsifying one's identity is easy and common.

1.5 The Test

A rule that everyone should exercise is to do a diligent background check on that person before you meet up with him or her for the first time, especially if you know nothing about that individual.

Start with a background check of their Facebook and social media accounts. Do they have many friends on Facebook? Are there strange posts or alarming pictures that bring suspicion? What about their LinkedIn, Twitter, Instagram, and other social media platforms?

If you feel that social media platforms do not provide enough information on that certain individual, then purchase an Internet background check. These background checks will tell you if an individual has had DUIs, bankruptcies, or criminal convictions, how many times they have been married, and even if they are late in paying their dog licenses, etc.

Once you find that person and feel there may be potential in the relationship but are unsure, you need to put them to the test. Yes, test. Not a written essay but what I like to call stress test situations.

Stressful situations and encounters can reveal a person's true character, so consider going out to a restaurant and observing how they treat the wait staff. Are they condescending or rude? Do they treat others with respect? Are they flirtatious? Do they keep looking at that beautiful person sitting at the other table?

Once the relationship has gained 1 year or more of traction, then take the testing to another level. One of my favorite situations that I like to advise is going on a trip with your companion. Bring a friend with you on the trip to give you a prospectus from outside your emotions.

Travel can be stressful; flights can be delayed and canceled, traffic is backed up for miles, hotels are overbooked, and, worst of all, baggage is lost or delayed. How does your companion handle the stress? Reactions in dealings with stress help in peeling back the layers of character flaws and the real nitty-gritty person.

If you are comfortable with the results of your testing and believe you have found someone you can grow and nurture a relationship with, strive to grow together as true friends. Be mindful of the needs of your companion and give them space when needed. They may want to be with their sister or hang with an old roommate. Try not to smother the other person. Space and brief separation at times are very healthy. Remember that healthy relationships require trust, communication, and respect.

Friendship is always a work in progress and never achieved overnight. True friends should be everyone's goal when it comes to a relationship and marriage. My wife and I are best friends, and yes, sometimes we do not see eye to eye. The key to overcoming conflicts is compromise and understanding. It's crucial to never go to bed angry with your friend, partner, or spouse. Always try to resolve any issues before bedtime and definitely before a business trip.

As 'distance makes the heart grow founder,' so does 'out of sight and out of mind' create a further riff in a relationship. Understand your partner's point of argument. Don't be pig-headed and stubborn just to get your way.

If you truly love your companion, you should be wise and understanding of their needs and come to a compromise. (More to follow in chapter two)

Happiness, wisdom, and understanding should be what we all strive for in our relationships.

Proverbs 3:13: *"Blessed are those who find wisdom, those who gain understanding."*

1.5 Summary

1. Don't be fooled. Marriage is something you always need to work at by understanding, respect, forgiveness, commitment, and faithfulness to your spouse.

2. Growing up and understanding who you are so you will know what you require in a relationship. Be honest with yourself about your needs and whether you are able to commit and work hard in a relationship so the relationship will grow and strengthen.

3. The best place to discover your soul mate is to seek common interests and activities.

4. Recognize the life partner that comes across your path and knows that's the one…

5. Seize that moment!

6. Testing the potential partner to see if he or she is the one and only one.

7. Friendship is always a work in progress and never, never achieved overnight.

8. Only with time will you really get to know your partner.

9. Understand your partner's needs.

10. Work on becoming wise and learning how to compromise to keep the peace.

Notes:

Chapter 2: Leap of Faith and Follow Your Heart

2.1 The Rules of Arguing

'__Proverbs 20:3__: *"It is to one's honor to avoid strife, but every fool is quick to quarrel."*

How wise and insightful is Proverbs 20:3. I believe the modern translation would say, "Drama has no room in a friendship, marriage and especially in a family."

In today's world, we already have so many negative distractions. Why add negativity to your relationship by dumping more garbage on it with criticism and disrespect? If you truly love, cherish and honor your spouse, then avoid negativity and drama!

2.2 The does and don'ts of arguing

But what happens when you do argue? How do you de-escalate the argument? Several checkpoints and rules need to be followed to avoid a complete meltdown of a relationship and marriage.

2.3 Respect

Follow the rules of arguing. In an argument, be respectful. Name-calling, cursing, and trying to humiliate your spouse only lead to greater strife and a very difficult road to healing the relationship. Two passages in the Bible come to mind, they are:

__Psalms 10:11__ - *"The mouth of the righteous is a fountain of life, but the mouth of the wicked conceals violence."* And,

Proverbs 15:1 - *"The words of the reckless pierce like swords, but the tongue of the wise brings healing..."*

2.3 Avoid changing your partner

Words can hurt for a lifetime and can cause irreversible damage in a relationship. When an argument becomes escalated, take a time out and collect your emotions; do this before you say the wrong thing. There are times to hold your ground and times to bite your tongue. You do not always need to be in the right. This is where compromise is important, and understanding the other side's view is the key to mending strife.

2.4 Stay on topic

Yes, we have all done it by bringing up some issue from the past that has no relevance to the argument. To guarantee further escalation than recall a certain circumstance that happened three years ago. "You said 'this' or did 'this,' and it hurt my feelings." Addressing issues immediately can prevent hurt feelings and resentment from festering over time. Bottling up and ignoring past hurts can lead to emotional outbursts during arguments and make it harder to resolve issues.

Proverbs 15:4: *"The soothing tongue is a tree of life, but a perverse tongue crushes the spirit."*

2.5 Empathy: Understand the other side's point of view

In some cases, that is very difficult to do, but in most cases, the other side may have some valid points. If you do realize you're in the wrong, then own up to it. Be an adult and admit your mistake. Always remember, the winner of these arguments should never rub the other's nose in the ground. Be a gracious winner and understand that it is difficult for the other side to admit defeat or wrongdoing.

2.6 Changing your partner

After months or years of courtship, you finally married that person, knowing they ate too fast or too slow. Those cute little indiscretions that you thought were hilarious are now annoying spousal habits. Understand that your partner has good and bad habits. Ask yourself if you can live with this person for the rest of your life knowing that they have these habits. Do a reality check and be honest with yourself before you take that vow. That person will or may not be changing his routine or actions. Keep in mind that sometimes trying to change your partners' habits may result in resentment. It is difficult for people to change lifelong habits. It takes time to change these habits, provided that they want to change.

I am a husband who is not the quickest person when getting out of the car. My wife, on the other hand, literally jumps out of the car when we have come to a stop in the parking space. I know it bugs her, and yes, she has made comments about my slow exit, but I do not take it to heart. Acceptance of who your spouse is relieves stressful pressures.

My wife has learned to accept and live with some of my innate habits. She has compromised instead of trying to change me and who I am.

2.7 Commitment

Matthew 19:4-6: *"He answered, "Have you not read that he who created them from the beginning made them male and female, and said, 'Therefore a man shall leave his father and his mother and hold fast to his wife, and the two shall become one*

14

flesh'? So, they are no longer two but one flesh. What therefore God has joined together let not man separate."

After 40 years of marriage, my wife and I are still close friends. However, I won't sugarcoat it - maintaining a healthy and happy marriage takes effort and perseverance, especially during tough times. In my experience, the key ingredients to a lasting and successful marriage are God, mutual respect, love, and commitment.

Commitment in marriage means not only being devoted to your partner but also being a supportive teammate who works hard to help out with daily responsibilities. This might mean getting off the couch and mowing the lawn, helping with childcare, cooking, cleaning, and organizing the household. Marriage is a partnership that requires teamwork, mutual support, and a willingness to go the extra mile for your loved one.

It's important to remember that the letter "I" is still present in the word "marriage." However, instead of focusing solely on individual needs, it's essential to shift the focus to what you can do for the betterment of the team. By prioritizing the success and happiness of the marriage as a whole, both partners can work together to overcome challenges and build a lasting, fulfilling relationship.

2.8 Growth

It is important to expect and embrace growth in your marriage, both as individuals and as a couple.

Individual growth can manifest in various ways, such as through increased maturity, personal development, and career progression. As we advance in our careers, we often take on greater responsibilities and climb the corporate ladder, from entry-level positions to assistant managers, managers, and potentially even executive roles like Vice President or higher. This growth requires perseverance, time, and personal development.

However, it's crucial to recognize that problems can arise in a relationship if one partner experiences career growth while the other does not. Feelings of envy, jealousy, and resentment can fester, creating tension and potentially damaging the relationship. It's important to acknowledge these negative emotions and work to address them together rather than allowing them to drive a wedge between you and your partner.

Galatians 5:26 *"Let us not become conceited, provoking one another, envying one another."*

In other words, be proud of your partner's successes and support their achievements. Your time will come. Just keep following the path the Lord has set in front of you, and all good things will be yours. Remember, you are a team, not everyone can score the touchdown, but the entire team brought that one player to the end zone.

Marriage growth in occupation is an individual goal that contributes to the marriage team. In most cases, households today, both spouses are the breadwinners for the family.

But what happens if one breadwinner outperforms the other partner? What happens if the wife brings home twice as much as the husband?

We have friends who had difficulties in their marriages when the wife was the major breadwinner. For one thing, men have been raised to be the provider. Men have been programmed to think they are the great hunter that goes out into the deep dark wilderness and hunts for food. Call it silly, but it's a fact that many males have a very difficult time dealing with their wives, making more money.

The added difficulty to our friend's issue was that the wife also made it known to others that she was the king contributor (or Queen contributor). This made our friend's marriage very shaky. Never, ever on both sides of the aisle should one or the other spouse boast and brag that they contribute to team marriage more. This action only sprouts contempt and humility.

The purpose of marriage is that both spouses grow together and contribute together (as much as the other can do for the team). Remember, it's you and your spouse alone in this big and competitive world. You need to have each other's back all the time. You are a 'Team.'

Growth in self-awareness is the other key to a successful marriage. Galatians nails this point in such simplicity.

Galatians 6:3 *"For if anyone thinks he is something when he is nothing, he deceives himself."*

In modern-day terms, my children would say, "be real."

Immaturity is another area that most men have an abundance of. I often hear how wives describe their husbands as immature and childish. I'm a perfect example of this. I still feel as though I am 18 years old. Good, bad, or indifferent, that is who I am.

Yes, it sometimes annoys the heck out of my wife, but I still play those silly pranks and goof off more than I should. The Bible says it best in the following:

1 Corinthians 13:11*: "When I was a child, I spoke like a child, I thought like a child, I reasoned like a child. When I became a man, I gave up childish ways."*

I have learned that when I push my wife's button once too often that I need to pull back before I get sent to the doghouse. I will attribute this to growth, becoming more mature, and understanding my wife's threshold.

Maturity and growth do not stop in one's silly actions, but maturity also includes your commitment and serious attitude to your marriage and your spouse. I'm not saying you should not have fun, but there is a time and place for everything.

2.9 Respect

Romans 12:10: *"Love one another with brotherly affection. Outdo one another in showing honor."*

Respect is one of the many keys to happiness, integrity, and a long-lasting relationship. If you take one thing from this book, it should be from **Romans 12:10** *"Outdo another in showing honor."* Roman's nails it right on the meaning of respect.

Here is a brief list of creating a better you and a better relationship by respecting others:

Do not judge others. *"Judge not, and you will not be judged."* **Luke 6:37**

Be positive to everyone. No one likes to be around a depressed, half-glass-empty type of personality.

1 Thessalonians 5:16: *"Rejoice always, pray without ceasing, give thanks in all circumstance; for this is the will of God in Christ Jesus for you."*

Do not gossip. Being a gossip is one of the most harmful habits a person can have. Not only does it spread negativity, but it also taints the intentions of others. Most people who gossip also enjoy drama.

"A dishonest man spreads strife, and a whisperer separates close friends." **Proverbs 20:19**

Be honest with everyone and yourself. You cannot respect others if you are not honest with them. You can't respect yourself if you are not honest with yourself. *"Lying lips are an abomination to the Lord, but those who act faithfully are his delight."* <u>Proverbs 12:22</u>

Love is the greatest of them all when it comes to respect. *"Let all that you do be done in love."* <u>1Corinthians 16:14</u>

Avoid a partner who flirts. Being flirtatious is the most disrespectful action anyone can be to his or her partner. It is immature, a complete disregard for the relationship or marriage, and an insult to your spouse and your family.

2.10 Work Hard

Working hard and striving to do your best is an essential aspect of personal growth and maturity.

Contribution to marriage goes beyond just financial support. Each member of the relationship should make important contributions in various aspects, such as household chores, nurturing and entertaining the children, cooking, cleaning, driving family members or kids, doing the laundry, providing emotional support, and most importantly, showing love. Whatever needs to be done should be done for the sake of your "team family."

Sharing responsibilities leads to a healthy and balanced relationship. On the other hand, when one partner is burdened with the majority of work and emotional support, the relationship becomes unbalanced, like a wheel that is out of balance and eventually deteriorates over time.

Emotional support is one of the most critical forms of support in a marriage. Are you always the one providing a listening ear or going the extra mile to make your partner happy without receiving anything in return?

Do you feel like emotional support is a one-way street where you are constantly giving and never receiving? When was the last time you asked your partner, "What can I do to help you?" or "How can I make it better?"

We all want to aid and comfort our companion, but to what limit? If, for months, even years, you are the individual that is always giving and never receiving, you will reach a breaking point. You have personal needs just like your partner. Let those needs be known. Holding issues inside of you will only fester to the point of eruption.

As I mentioned before, self-awareness is key to a healthy relationship. Having this awareness about yourself (taking too much from your partner or always giving to your partner with nothing in return) shows signs of maturity, caring, and loving.

Understand that there are requirements for achieving balance in a relationship. Relationship balance requires open communication and a strong effort to listen to your companion and act to your partner's needs.

So, which one are you, a receiver or a giver? Or are you an understanding partner that provides both attributes? If you and your partner have these two healthy and mature traits, then your relationship is stronger than most other relationships. Strive to be understanding, kind, generous, respectful, forgiving, compromising, and loving.

Ephesians 4:32: *"Be kind and compassionate to one another, forgiving each other, just as in Christ God forgave you."*

Selflessness is the best way to describe what we all should be in our lives and relationships. Choose others over yourself, especially the ones you love. Not only will you nurture and strengthen your relationship, but also you will feel better about yourself and become a better person.

Ephesians 4:29: *"Do not let any unwholesome talk come out of your mouths, but only what is helpful for building others up according to their needs, that it may benefit those who listen."*

Make an effort every day to help others and be a blessing, especially to your companion.

Our tongue and our actions can heal and hurt. We all have been disappointed in one way or another by our partner thru actions or words. We have also disappointed our partner. Either way, relationships need to be worked out when disappointments arise.

Overcoming disappointment requires communication. Be bold and communicate immediately what the specific disappointment was. Do not suppress or ignore your partner's actions. If you are disappointed and put off addressing the action, your partner will keep disappointing you, leading to relationship erosion.

2.11 Summary

1. In an argument, be respectful.
2. Stay on topic.
3. Understand the other side's point of view.
4. Avoid changing who your partner is.
5. Commitment to the marriage.
6. Marriage is teamwork
7. Growth, individually and as partners.
8. Respect each other's wishes.
9. Work Hard and do your best for yourself and your partner.

Notes:

Chapter 3: Communication within the Marriage

3.1 Communication Overview for Marriage

God has given us the ability to communicate in several ways. One way is verbal the other way is through actions. The primary way to communicate is through words. God made the use of words a tool for us to build up and also to tear down.

The world came into existence because God spoke it into being (**Genesis 1:** *"And God said... "*). *"And God blessed them,"* the Bible says after creating Adam and Eve. *"And God said to them, 'Be fruitful and multiply, and fill the earth... "* 'Genesis 1:28,'

While words are crucial and account for a more significant portion of our communication, they are insufficient for effective biblical communication. God encourages us not to rely solely on words for communication. Consider **1 John 3:18,** which says, *"Little children, let us love one another in action and truth, not in word or mouth."* Deeds must accompany our words. *"Your actions speak so loudly that I can't hear what you're saying,"* as the old saying goes. This statement contains a lot of truth!

However, we cannot demonstrate love solely by our acts because God tells us hundreds of times in the Bible that He loves us. As a result, we should not only do things to show our love for others but also improve our ability to tell others that we love them and use well-chosen words to communicate, solve, or prevent problems.

The importance of communication in a marriage cannot be over-emphasized. Your communication can either build or undermine your marriage, depending on how well you communicate. As a necessity, you must exercise extreme caution in what you say and how you say it with your partner. Love your partner, and make sure that your words reflect that love.

Matthew 12:35: *"A good man brings good things out of the good stored up in him, and an evil man brings evil things out of the evil stored up in him. Bless and enlighten others with your words."*

Your remarks should encourage and uplift your partner and those around you. To interact in a Christ-like manner, the well-being of others must take precedence over your desires. (Ephesians 4:29; Romans 15:2, 14:19.)

Active listening is among the most important parts of communication.

Respect, honor, and love are communicated to your spouse through active listening. When one or both couples try to talk before taking the time to understand the other, the communication typically goes south. Proverbs could not have said this any better.

Proverbs 18:13: *"He who answers a matter before he hears it- It is folly and shame to him."*

Your words can either build up and bless you or tear you down and hurt you. Make no negative, harsh, or insulting remarks to your spouse or others about your spouse.

James 3:5: *"Likewise, the tongue is a small part of the body, but it makes great boasts. ... Consider what a great forest is set on fire by a small spark."*

Make time for excellent communication with your partner a top priority. I found that when my wife and I have an open line of communication and try to understand each other's points of view, our arguments seem to be resolved very easily. We walk away feeling fulfilled and loved because the other understands our point.

It's easy to get caught up in life's commitments and expectations and overlook the significance of maintaining regular communication with your spouse. Over time, different degrees of communication will emerge. However, be conscious of the depth of your communication and ensure that there are opportunities to go beyond surface-level communication.

Matthew 6:31: *"So do not worry, saying, 'What shall we eat?' or 'What shall we drink? For the pagans run after all these things, and your heavenly Father knows that you need."*

In a marriage, communication with God is essential. This practice builds a spiritual connection while also deepening your ties with God. When you pray and spend time with God, try to find a quiet and tranquil location. Also, praying with your spouse can make you feel closer in spirit and love for each other. Placing God at the center of your marriage can help your bond grow between you, God, and your partner.

It's surprising to learn that many Christian couples have never prayed alone with their spouse. It's important to have alone time and pray together to enrich the soul and strengthen the bond between you and your spouse. **James 4:8 says**, *"Come near to God, and he will come near to you."* Having God in the center of your relationship is the greatest thing you can do for your marriage.

Couples in healthy marriages are open and honest with each other, but they should not use "honesty" as an excuse to hurt or criticize each other. Remember, your words have power, and they can leave a permanent wound. Honesty is important, but it should not be used as a tool of cruelty. **Ephesians 4:25 says,** *"Therefore each of you must put off falsehood and speak truthfully to your neighbor, for we are all members of one body."*

1 John 2:16: *"For all that is in the world, the lust of the flesh and the eyes and the boastful pride of life, is not from the Father, but is from the world."*

I find that the "Hollywood Tribe" exemplifies the term "self-deception." How many marriages in the Hollywood circus have failed? How many actors and actresses are on their 3rd, 4th, and 5th marriages? I bring this question up to show that Hollywood characters are prime examples of self-deception. Most, not all, actors and actresses, producers, directors, media executives, rock stars, agents, etc., think so highly of themselves that they lose touch with who they are. They live in a fantasy world that they believe revolves around them. Don't get me wrong; there are a lot of very wealthy business executives that have this same flaw. I'm not judging, but I am pointing out a transparent observation. And yes, there are good people in these industries trying to maintain a moral compass.

Paul wrote in Ephesians that sin is disruptive and corruptive. How can a marriage survive when you have a partner that carries traits of self-deception, manipulation, ego, self-centeredness, narcissism, dishonesty, conceitedness, and have a love and desire for power and money?

The Book of Mathew points out that you cannot be with God and also with the world.

Mathew 6:24 *"No one can serve two masters, for either he will hate one and love the other, or he will be devoted to the one and despise the other. You cannot serve God and money."*

Understand and identify these sinful traits early on in a relationship to avoid ending up miserable.

Summary

1. Two types of communication: Verbal and non-verbal
2. Encourage and uplift your partner.
3. Bring God into your communication.
4. Honesty should not be used as a tool for guilty.
5. Sin in a marriage is disruptive and corruptive.

Notes:

Chapter 4: Different Levels of Communication

Communication has different levels ranging from non-verbal to deep intimacy level of communication. The higher the level of communication in your marriage, the better the chances of experiencing a wonderful and loving relationship. Looking back at the start of our marriage, I can see that our communication level was low, but now we have achieved a deep and intimate relationship. It doesn't have to take over 40 years of marriage to reach this level of communication; by practicing and being open and honest, you can accelerate the process in a matter of months or years with your spouse.

It can be challenging to reveal your inner self to someone, especially if you have had past relationships that ended in heartbreak. The fear of being too vulnerable and opening yourself up to potential hurt and disappointment can be overwhelming. A broken heart is one of the most painful emotional experiences, and it can take years to heal from.

Remember what Jesus taught us:

"Jesus said unto him, Thou shalt love the Lord thy God with all thy heart, and with all thy soul, and with all thy mind. This is the first and great commandment. And the second is like unto it, Thou shalt love thy neighbor as thyself. On these two commandments hang all the law and the prophets."

And what John wrote in the book of Romans:

Romans 14:19: *"So then let us pursue what makes for peace* *and for mutual upbuilding."*

Jesus and Paul have taught us to "love our neighbor" and "pursue what makes peace and mutual upbuilding." Communication plays a vital role in achieving these teachings. The type and depth of communication we have with our partner can greatly influence the quality of our relationship. While superficial communication may suffice for casual acquaintances, deeper communication is necessary for a fulfilling marriage.

In some marriages, communication may be limited to the exchange of surface-level facts and information. However, personal and intimate communication is essential for establishing a strong and lasting bond. Being truly known and understood by our spouse is one of the greatest blessings of marriage.

While deep communication can be challenging for some individuals, it is necessary to build trust and honesty in the relationship.

Improving communication in a marriage requires active listening and understanding our partner's perspectives and emotions. As the saying goes, "You have one mouth and two ears," so we should listen twice as much as we speak.

Below I have listed levels of communication that I felt and have experienced in my marriage. Review these levels of communication and discuss with your partner how you communicate at each level. Can your communication improve individually and together?

4.1 Surface Communication

Is your communication just about the facts, nothing deep only surface exposure? The surface level of communication entails sharing facts or information with the least amount of vulnerability and intimacy. This type of communication occurs at the beginning of a relationship; unfortunately, some couples never get past this stage of communication.

At this level, conversations may revolve around the weather, daily schedules, work, or gossip. While there may be some joking and goofing around, there is no real substance to the discussion.

If you find that your communication is limited to this level, it's time to take action. Start by discussing your concerns and views about your relationship, and don't be afraid to reveal more of yourself. For example, you could talk about how a sermon impacted you or share your thoughts on the current and future state of your partnership.

Developing a deeper connection requires honesty, transparency, and a willingness to listen and understand each other's perspectives. Don't wait until minor conflicts become major issues; address them as they arise, and work together to find a resolution.

To improve your communication individually and as a couple, start by praying together and inviting God into your marriage. As you grow in your relationship with each other and with God, you will find that your communication will naturally deepen, leading to a stronger, more fulfilling bond. Remember, a happy wife is a happy life, and the same holds true for husbands. By sharing your thoughts, opinions, and desires with each other, you can build a foundation of mutual respect and understanding that will last a lifetime.

4.2 Communication with Mutual Sharing

Our respect and love grew stronger when my wife and I started sharing personal preferences, beliefs, concerns, desires, and experiences. We began discussing our personal challenges, memories, goals, and so on. I noticed that at this stage, we began to tackle issues together and strengthen our "Team Marriage."

Additionally, we began to discuss physical intimacy, which is an essential topic to address. It may feel uncomfortable at first, but it's important to understand each other's needs and find ways to improve each other's desires.

Through mutual sharing, respect for one another will flourish and grow. Respect is a crucial element in building a long-lasting marriage. We will discuss respect in more detail later in the book.

It is important to note that reaching this level of communication takes time, effort, and vulnerability. But the benefits of mutual sharing are worth it. Your relationship will become stronger, and you will develop a deeper understanding and appreciation of each other.

So, take the time to have these conversations with your partner and continue to build a strong foundation for your marriage.

4.3 The 'All Of Me Level' of Communication

Galatians 5:13 *"For you were called to freedom, brothers. Only do not use your freedom as an opportunity for the flesh, but through love, serve one another."*

My wife and I felt a great feeling of freedom when we opened up completely. It took about three years into our marriage to achieve this level. When we had our first child, we were both working and climbing the corporate ladder. Needless to say, there was a lot of stress in our marriage.

What got us through these challenging times was opening up ourselves and communicating our expectations, concerns, needs, and anxieties. Raising children can be very stressful, especially when both parents are working. Communication is key to getting through the stress and daily emotional rollercoaster. Express your emotions if you feel you are carrying the majority of the child-rearing responsibilities—nothing worst as a parent that is burning out emotionally.

Communicate that you need a break. Taking a hot bath, going to the gym, having time by yourself and enjoying a good book, taking a long walk to collect yourself, or having a date night with your partner, are some things to reenergize your spirit and your relationship.

You will know when you hit the "The All Of Me" level by completely having an open line of dialogue and feeling that your inner soul is on the table. This can be a very emotional event. You may experience crying and even anger. It is so important to keep your emotions in check and look into the success of achieving an open line of communication.

You and your partner can express your inner thoughts, anxieties, preferences, loves, and dislikes here. The discussion may include heartfelt emotional displays and revealing inner thoughts, ideas, and experiences. Not only do discussions at this level assist a couple in becoming more intimate, but it also helps with conflicts, decision-making, child-rearing, and communicating problems with resolutions. When you and your spouse discuss thoughts and feelings in an open, loving, and respectful environment, issues can be resolved more easily and successfully.

According to studies on the importance of self-disclosure, couples who open up to each other about their thoughts and feelings tend to have happier relationships. It's important to note that couples often mirror each other's level of disclosure, so if one spouse withholds information, the other may follow suit. Creating an environment where both partners can communicate openly and positively is crucial for building and maintaining a strong relationship.

If you notice your spouse withdrawing and not communicating openly, it's important to address the issue and your concerns. However, timing is key. Consider your partner's state of mind and whether it's a good time to discuss sensitive issues. Wait for a moment when they are in a more receptive mood.

It's also important to remember that when one partner is discussing their issues, the other should listen actively without interrupting. Give your partner your full attention and show that you are genuinely interested in what they have to say. This will encourage them to be more open and honest in their communication with you.

4.4 Communication and Personality

Spouses often differ in their communication style in terms of quality and quantity. Knowing and understanding each other's personalities can aid in this aspect. One simple way to determine communication style is by the length of time spent talking and being together. There are two types of communicators: outgoing and inward.

Outgoing communicators tend to talk more, give detailed information, and dislike silence. In contrast, inward communicators limit their communication, preferring to use fewer words and stick to essential ideas or facts. Inward communicators may frustrate outgoing communicators with their limited information sharing. Understanding your partner's communication style is important in achieving a closer relationship.

We have encountered many couples where one partner is extremely outgoing while the other is more reserved, almost like they are complete opposites. However, our "Polar-Opposite" friends tend to experience more issues and drama than couples who share similar communication styles. Nonetheless, we have noticed that our friends overcame their differences by showing abundant respect and compromise towards each other.

The outgoing partner made a conscious effort to listen more and limit interruptions when their partner was speaking. Meanwhile, the more reserved partner worked on communicating in greater detail and expressing their feelings in a more personal way. It's worth noting that this couple received marriage counseling to enhance their communication skills and build their relationship.

When partners are outgoing and verbal, they tend to have regular and active dialogues. My wife and I are both outgoing, and we found that our communication improved as we expressed our concerns and feelings. However, it's crucial to avoid speaking over each other. My wife and I learned to take turns speaking and listening, and we made a conscious effort to enhance our listening skills continually.

4.5 Two Inward Communicating Couples

When both partners have difficulty communicating or are more inward in personality, their conversations tend to be pleasant, specific, and to the point. However, they might avoid discussing important issues that need to be addressed. These individuals tend to avoid conflict and have a tendency to take constructive criticism personally, which can be detrimental to their relationship.

To become better communicators, inward couples need to understand their communication style and make a conscious effort to be more open with their expressions, needs, and wants in their relationship. They also need to develop a thicker skin and avoid taking their partner's opinions as personal attacks. By being receptive to their partner's feedback and working together to improve their communication, inward couples can strengthen their relationship and build a more fulfilling partnership.

4.6 Non-Verbal Communicate in a Marriage

Ephesians 4: 1-3: *"I therefore, a prisoner for the Lord, urge you to walk in a manner worthy of the calling to which you have been called, 2. with all humility and gentleness, with patience, bearing with one another in love, 3. eager to maintain the unity of the Spirit in the bond of peace."*

Communication doesn't always require the use of words. Non-verbal communication, also known as "body language," can express a wide range of emotions without speaking a single word. Body language can convey emotions such as happiness, anger, frustration, boredom, acceptance, disgust, and even love. However, it's important to be mindful of the messages you are sending through your body language and silence. Knowing when to "hold your tongue" is crucial to understanding the message you are conveying.

Silence can allow another person to interpret your message, which may or may not be accurate. It's understandable to take some time to reflect and gather your thoughts before discussing a problem, but giving your spouse the "silent treatment" can be emotionally abusive.

Appropriate assertiveness and asking for clarification when unsure of your partner's communication through actions or silence are important. Asking your partner to express their emotions and thoughts is preferable to making assumptions. We are not mind readers, and assuming what our partner is thinking can lead to disastrous misunderstandings and further escalate an argument.

4.7 Select your words with care

Proverbs 25:11: *"A word fitly spoken is like apples of gold in* *a setting of silver."*

Words can both create and destroy. Communicate in a way that strengthens and improves your relationship.

Effective communication requires a combination of grace and truth. It's important to express the truth with compassion and love. Without these elements, a blunt statement can come across as harsh and insensitive, such as saying, "My mother's cooking is much better than yours." This type of communication can seriously damage a relationship and cause hurt feelings. On the other hand, trying to be overly positive and avoiding the truth can also be harmful. If you pretend to love a dish when you really don't, you're setting yourself up for a lifetime of unpleasant meals.

If you communicated with the right attitude and complemented by the elements listed below, there's a significant probability that you're communicating successfully and efficiently.

4.8 The Dos In Marriage Communication

The following is a list of **"Do's and Don'ts"** required in becoming a better communicator:

Keep working on these <u>Dos</u>:

A. Sensitivity:

"Words can cut like a knife." You may have heard this saying before. I have friends who are in their late 60s and still recall hurtful words from a parent or friends during their youth. It is important to be mindful and sensitive to what you say. Show self-control, kindness, and care even when being sarcastic, especially during arguments or when trying to make a point.

As **Frederick Douglass** once said, *"It is easier to build strong* *children than to repair broken men.*" We are all God's perfect children, so don't be the one who contributes to the devil's plan by breaking down your partner's spirit.

B. Understanding:

When I think of understanding, I think of '**empathy**.'

Webster's dictionary defines empathy as: "the action of understanding, being aware of, being sensitive to, and vicariously experiencing the feelings, thoughts, and experience of another of either the past or present without having the feelings, thoughts, and experience fully communicated in an objectively *explicit manner.*"

Being aware of your actions and understanding and having sensitivity to your partner's feelings is the strength and bond of a healthy marriage. My wife and I have grown and strengthened our empathy for each other, our children, our family, and our friends over the years. It seems that with the growth of empathy, we have also grown as Christians.

I encourage you and your partner to really explore how you can improve your understanding of each other through empathy. By doing so, I believe that your communication with each other will improve, and your respect for each other will be strengthened.

C. Love:

1 Corinthians 13:4-5: *"Love is patient, love is kind. It does not envy, it does not boast, it is not proud. It does not dishonor others, it is not self-seeking, it is not easily angered, it keeps no record of wrongs."*

1 Corinthians 13:4-5 perfectly describes love. It's amazing how we can feel the love in someone's heart even when they are strangers to us. **"Love is kind,"** and as Christians who follow and worship Jesus Christ, we should show love not only to our spouse, children, and family but also to strangers. Love is the essence of

being a Christian.

Always communicate with your partner in a loving and caring way. Even when you have a disagreement, never forget to hold on to the love that you have in your heart. With love in your heart, you allow God to intervene, but without it, you leave room for the devil to tear away at the fiber of your relationship and your spirit. Satan delights in strife, envy, gossip, drama, animosity, hatred, and the lack of love. Do not allow the forces of darkness to take hold in your life. Instead, be strong, keep God in your life, read the Bible, belong to a Bible-based church, and never stop praying and worshiping Jesus, the Lord of truth, light, joy, happiness, and love.

D. Clarity:

Clear and concise communication is crucial in any relationship, especially when it comes to disagreements and arguments. Stick to the relevant facts and avoid going off on tangents that distract from the main point. It's also important to resist the urge to bring up past issues that are not relevant to the current situation. Doing so can create unnecessary tension and make it difficult to move forward. Instead, focus on addressing the specific problem at hand and finding a resolution that works for both parties.

E. Honor and Respect:

Whom do you honor, who do you respect that is on this earth? The answer better be your partner. Your partner deserves all the honor and respect from you. Honoring your partner and showing respect will show your children how they must treat their future partner and others.

In today's world, honoring your partner is hard to find, especially with younger couples. Why is that? Is it because many of these younger couples never had the family experience where their parents honored each other?

Today the divorce rate averages approximately 9.5% of married couples for 2021. However, over 19 million children are living in single-parent households or approximately 25% of the children in the United States.

These stats do not make it any easier for children to grow up and experience the honor and respect adult parents should have for each other. Children must learn respect from the actions of their parents, even if the parents are divorced. We lead by example! The way you treat others is a clear indication of how your children will learn respect and honor.

Single parents and other family members must make a concentrated effort to guide and correct their children regarding respecting and honoring others.

If you are divorced, make sure you place your children first by showing respect to your ex-partner. Never speak ill of them, never speak of the hurt you experienced, and always bite your tongue when the thought arises of sharing your misfortune. When your children become teenagers, they will understand the truth about their parents and arrive at their own conclusion.

Philippians 2:3: *"Do nothing from rivalry or conceit but in humility count others more significant than yourselves."*

Respect others as you want to be respected. This is key in a marriage, friendship, the work environment, and every day-to-day encounter.

I've noticed that many elderly couples that have been married for 25 years or more seem to lose respect for each other. Sometimes this respect erodes to the point of divorce.

It's astonishing to me that some couples that have been married for over 30 years are in the process of getting a divorce. They've spent approximately one-quarter of their life with that special person, and now they have ill will and contempt in their heart.

From my observation, the main factor was respect no longer existed between the couples. The partnership became toxic by relentless nagging, sarcasm, drama, and even verbal abuse.

Who wants to be in a relationship with all that negative energy between them? So it is important to always ask God for humility and respect for others. Ask yourself, would you want to be the receiver of blunt, nagging, and hurtful words?

With the first signs of dishonor in the marriage, take action and address the issue with your partner. The forces of darkness want nothing more than to see a happy, loving marriage erode and disintegrate into hate and animosity.

F. Honesty and Integrity:

2 Corinthians 8:21: *"For we are taking pains to do what is right, not only in the eyes of the Lord but also in the eyes of man."*

It is not easy to be a Christian. The Bible points this out in multiple scriptures. The strongest directive was from Jesus when he said, *"If any of you want to be my followers, you must forget about yourself. You must take up your cross every day and follow me. (Luke 9:23)*

As Christians, we acknowledge that we are human and prone to sin. Therefore, we must strive for honesty and integrity every day. We are ambassadors of God's children and must work hard to demonstrate honesty and integrity in all our actions, as our children, neighbors, and partners are constantly observing us.

Unfortunately, the foundation of honesty and integrity is what the devil loves to attack. The accuser wants us to believe that we are unworthy of God's grace because of our sins. Before we know it, we may give up and say, **"I'm such a sinner. God will never**

41

love or forgive me."

However, the truth is the opposite: God will always love us. In God's eyes, we are His masterpiece, His perfect creation. Consider the highlighted individuals in the Bible and their sins and wrong decisions. Despite their flaws, God still loved them and forgave them.

The first sin of the bible was when Eve defied God's commandment not to eat the fruit. What did she do? She deliberately ignored God and ate the fruit, and then convinced Adam to do the same. Adam ate the fruit, knowing what God had forbidden. God forgave them, and Eve became the first mother to the world.

King David committed adultery, murder, deception, and lies, yet he became one of the great leaders in the Bible. However, he repented and asked God for forgiveness, which he received.

Noah, who was a drunkard, was chosen by God to build the Ark and save the earth from the great flood.

Moses had a violent temper and even killed a man, but he repented and became one of God's most humble servants. His transformation serves as a testament to God's unwavering love and unlimited forgiveness.

Solomon, David's son, was chosen by God to rule Israel, but he turned away from God and worshipped false idols due to his many distractions, including his 700 wives. Despite his mistakes, God forgave him and allowed him to remain the King of Israel for the rest of his life.

Peter, one of Jesus' closest friends and apostles, denied knowing Jesus three times. However, Jesus forgave him, and he became one of the greatest Christian teachers.

Saul (Paul) persecuted and killed Christians before Jesus

appeared to him and touched his spirit with forgiveness and love. Paul then became an instrumental figure in teaching millions of people about the gospel and the Christian faith.

These biblical leaders show us that becoming a Christian doesn't mean we will never sin. The Christian life is a constant battle between the Spirit and the flesh, which will continue until our last breath on this earth.

As Christians, we will go to heaven to be with our heavenly Father when we die. Jesus taught us that we will receive new bodies that will never be corrupted by sin, just like His resurrected body.

1 Corinthian: 15 20-28: *"But Christ has indeed been raised from the dead, the first fruits of those who have fallen asleep. 21 For since death came through a man, the resurrection of the dead comes also through a man. 22 For as in Adam all die, so in Christ, all will be made alive. 23 But each in turn: Christ, the first fruits; then, when he comes, those who belong to him. 24 Then the end will come when he hands over the kingdom to God the Father after he has destroyed all dominion, authority, and power. 25 For he must reign until he has put all his enemies under his feet. 26 The last enemy to be destroyed is death. 27 For he "has put everything under his feet. "Now, when it says that "everything" has been put under him, it is clear that this does not include God himself, who put everything under Christ. 28 When he has done this, then the Son himself will be made subject to him who put everything under him, so that God may be all in all."*

Jesus wants you to be with him for eternity. Just ask, and you will receive. If our Heavenly Father can forgive Paul and the other heroes in the Bible, he can certainly forgive you.

G. Self-Control:

<u>2 Timothy 1:7</u>: *"For God gave us a spirit not of fear but of power and love and self-control."*

Jesus teaches us that it is not enough to just have peace; we also need to work on keeping our peace daily. In other words, "Self-Control" is the key to keeping peace consistently every day, every hour, and every minute in our lives.

Do not verbalize everything that is on your mind. Especially in an argument, think before you speak. Saying something that you will regret later can be avoided by just controlling your tongue. Keeping your emotions in check thru self-control leads to inner peace. You cannot expect to have your emotions run wild and yet have peace in your life. God has given us the ability and strength to control these emotions. Are you the one that gets irritated or angry in traffic, or does a rainy weekend ruin your outdoor activity? These are things that you cannot control. Rise above those irritating and uncontrollable inconveniences by asking God to strengthen your inner peace and control your feelings.

Coming home, do you dump all the work garbage and unload it on your spouse or family? We all have had those days when nothing goes right. The last thing you want to do is unload that garbage on your marriage. You need to leave all the negativity at the workplace. Build self-control by practicing coming home and making a conscious effort not to speak about the day's negativity. Put a smile on your face and be grateful for the gifts God has given you.

Your goal should be to strengthen your marriage every day by being positive, upbeat, and fun to be around. This way, your partner, family, children, and even your pets will look forward to seeing you when you walk through the front door. How do you leave the negativity at work and not bring it home, or how do you just beat the negative garbage thrown at you daily? There are many habits that you can develop so you can overcome the garbage pile. The first habit is to find a peaceful and quiet spot (away from work, away from the negative people) and read and meditate on bible verses. This is very easy to do in today's world of technology. Download apps on your smartphone that will give you daily inspirational spiritual messages. Listen to spiritual podcasts daily on the radio. Another way to get right with your emotional feelings is to read your bible at lunch breaks or before you begin the trip home from work. Every morning I wake up and read a scripture that has been sent to me via email. There are dozens of pastors that have this free daily email.

I look forward to reading these morning emails; it starts my day with biblical inspiration and the joy and love of Jesus.

I also have found that limiting your news information is also helpful. With today's news about unrest, pandemics, political circus clowns, the economy, and mandates, it is easy to head down the rabbit hole of emotional negativity. Practice self-control with the news input in your daily life. Bring God back into your life when you feel the world's garbage being dumped on you. Nothing ever good comes from being a person who rides the emotional roller coaster with drama, spite, and negative emotions.

Negative feelings or losing your temper is a sign that you have lost control of your emotions. Telling someone off, running around all depressed, and even having the whoa-is-me pity party clearly indicate that your emotions are controlling you rather than you controlling your life. Emotional roller coasters can lead to you saying something hurtful and regretful to your partner. Achieve self-control to avoid the pitfalls of negative feelings in your relationship. Remember, you are part of a **team marriage**. There is no room in your team's lineup for negativity, the lack of self-control, or the pity-of-me attitude.

If the following factors accompany or characterize your words, actions, and attitude, you are most likely engaging in **"corrupt communication."**

Ephesians 4:29: *"Let no corrupting talk come out of your mouths, but only such as is good for building up, as fits the occasion, that it may give grace to those who hear."*

4.9 The Don'ts In Marriage Communication

The following are the "Don'ts" in communications:

A. Criticizing:

Criticism can be detrimental to a marriage, as it can gradually erode the emotional connection between partners. When criticism becomes a habitual pattern, it can overwhelm the spouse and create a negative atmosphere in the relationship. It is essential to examine our words and determine whether they are critical or lacking positivity, praise, and love.

It is crucial to infuse peace, joy, love, and positivity in our communication with our partners. Our words have the power to build or destroy, and therefore, we should be intentional about what we say. We should remember that our words are like seeds; if we sow weeds, we will reap weeds. However, if we plant seeds of positivity, we will enjoy a flourishing and harmonious relationship.

B. Nagging / Strife:

Constant nagging opens the door to bitterness and strife. The Bible teaches us that we must avoid opening the door to the darkness of evil. Satan's pleasure is seeing a crack develop in marriage through constant nagging, drama, bitterness, and strife. That small crack in a marriage will lead to a larger crack and then eventually a crack the size of the Grand Canyon.

Jesus said in **Mark 3:25:** *"A home filled with strife and division destroys itself."*

C. Quarreling:

Proverbs 21:19: *"It is better to live in a desert land than with a quarrelsome and fretful woman."*

The destructive force of nagging, strife, and constant quarreling can tear apart a marriage. Sadly, I have witnessed this in the lives of many friends whose marriages have ended in a bitter divorce. However, there are ways to avoid quarreling and build a healthy relationship. One such way is to talk through problems and strive to understand each other's perspectives.

Another effective solution is to seek Christian marriage counseling, where a professional can provide guidance and support in resolving conflicts and improving communication. It is essential to recognize that a harmonious and peaceful marriage is like a sports team that functions optimally when there is unity and cooperation.

As an individual, you will experience greater happiness when there is peace in your family. Your family will flourish in love, and your children will carry the legacy of your family's love into their own future families. Remember, the most effective way to teach your children is by setting a positive example through your own behavior. Therefore, strive to promote love, peace, family unity, and Christian values in your marriage.

D. Faultfinding:

Faultfinding is another way that marriages become destroyed. If you want your marriage to succeed, then you need to search for the positive qualities that your partner has. Finger-pointing and the blame game will only tear down your marriage. Take responsibility and avoid criticism and blaming your partner. Rise above the negativity that fault finding is and accept that your partner is not perfect, and neither are you.

John 8:7: *"And as they continued to ask him, he stood up and said to them, "Let him who is without sin among you be the first to throw a stone at her."*

E. Comparing your spouse to others:

Proverbs 18-22: *"He who finds a wife finds a good thing and obtains favor from the Lord."*

You married your spouse because they were one of a kind. They made you happy inside. You loved being in love; you looked forward to spending all of your time with them. And now, years into your marriage, you see others and compare your partner to them.

Let me tell you that the grass is never greener on the other side of the fence. Your wandering eyes and false ideology will create strife and ill will in your marriage. Be happy and content with what God has blessed you with. God has blessed you with people, including your life partner, to come into your life. The Bible says it over and over again that "We need one another." You will be able to accomplish more, grow stronger, and achieve a lifetime of blessings in "Team Marriage." "You are in it to win it." Meaning your partner and you are in life's fast lane to win. Don't let outside forces and distractions tear your team apart.

F. Jealousy and being overly sensitive:

James 3:14-15: ESV *"But if you have bitter jealousy and selfish ambition in your hearts, do not boast and be false to the truth. This is not the wisdom that comes down from above, but is earthly, unspiritual, demonic."*

How many relationships does a jealous partner destroy? In most cases, jealousy is not even warranted; it's just a figment of imagination. Jealousy is an impulse from a festering negative mindset of insecurity and careless suspicion. Jealousy can be a destructive force in a relationship, causing the accused partner to feel powerless and ultimately leading to the demise of the relationship. It is important to be aware of possessive characteristics in future partners, as they may be rooted in feelings of inadequacy and low self-esteem. Initially, a jealous person's actions may be seen as cute or caring, but it is important to recognize the red flags that indicate a potentially toxic relationship.

I have personally experienced the negative effects of dating a jealous person. In the beginning, I did not notice the warning signs, such as her going through my personal belongings. As time went on, her jealousy escalated to the point where she would question my every move and demand to know where I was at all times. I felt suffocated and trapped by her controlling behavior and realized that it would only get worse if we were to continue the relationship. The breaking point came when she showed up unannounced late at night, accusing me of being with someone else. It was then that I knew the relationship had to end. I learned that there is no room for jealousy in a healthy relationship or marriage. It is important to understand your partner's insecurities and level of self-security before committing to a long-term relationship.

G. Lying:

Revelation 21:8: *"But as for the cowardly, the faithless, the detestable, as for murderers, the sexually immoral, sorcerers, idolaters, and all liars, their portion will be in the lake that burns with fire and sulfur, which is the second death."*

And

1 John 2:4: *"Whoever says, "I know him" but does not keep his commandments is a liar, and the truth is not in him."*

And

1 Peter 3:7: *"Likewise, husbands, live with your wives in an understanding way, showing honor to the women as the weaker vessel, since they are heirs with you of the grace of life, so that your prayers may not be hindered."*

And

Ephesians 5:33: *"However, let each one of you love his wife as himself, and let the wife see that she respects her husband."*

And

Ephesians 5:31: *"Therefore a man shall leave his father and mother and hold fast to his, and the two shall become one flesh."*

There are so many great and informative scriptures about respect, honor, loyalty, sin, and marriage.

Ephesians 5:31, for me, emphasizes that in marriage, a husband's priority should be his wife and the family they create together, forming a united "Team Marriage." Being on a team means having each other's backs, striving for each other's success, and putting the needs of the team before one's own. This is exemplified in sports and in the military, where teammates and soldiers rely on each other for survival and success. Similarly, in a marriage, being a part of a Team Marriage involves being loyal, honest, and supportive of one's spouse. However, when one partner begins to lie, cheat, or act selfishly, the foundation of Team Marriage begins to crumble. Little white lies can turn into full-blown deception, eroding trust and respect within the relationship. Deceitful behavior shows a lack of concern for one's partner's emotions and feelings and can ultimately lead to the downfall of the marriage.

Furthermore, some individuals begin to believe their own lies, creating a distorted reality they can no longer differentiate from the

50

truth. This self-centered mentality can damage relationships with family, friends, and romantic partners. For example, we had a single guy move into our neighborhood. I met him one day while walking our dog. He seemed like a very pleasant person. As time passed, I ran into him at the grocery store and in the neighborhood. One day at the gym, we crossed paths and began a lengthy conversation about who we were, where we came from, our likes, and what sports teams we rooted for... Guy talk. In conversing with my new neighbor, he enlightened me on how he was divorced and not speaking to his wife. He also mentioned that he does not speak to his mother, father, or younger brother. It seemed that he was at odds with most of his family, his ex-wife, and past friendships. He made a comment that enlightened me on who he really is and what his inner core feelings and beliefs were. His comment was, **"My family and friends are all messed up. My mother and father are clowns, my brother is a clown, and most of all, my old friends are clowns."** Reflecting on the conversations I had with him in the past, all his comments were 'me,' 'I,' and 'Whoa is me.' I could see that he was extremely self-centered, and the world evolved around him. No way any of his soured relations could have anything to do with him!

I asked him about his marriage. He went on to explain that his wife could not bear the responsibility of being married. He explained that she became a nagging wife, especially after he came home from the gym, golf, or a business trip. She nagged him relentlessly! They had one daughter, and it sounded as if he did very little to help in raising their toddler and helping around the house. He commented, "It was the wife's responsibility to clean and take care of the home and children." Please note that his wife also had a full-time job. He even bragged to me how he was ranked number 5, in the nation, on a war-type video game. I do not play video games, but I do know for anyone to be ranked that high on one of the most popular video games, you need to spend a lot of time practicing and playing, usually on the couch by yourself.

My point of this story is that my new neighbor believed he was always in the right and never the one to be at fault. He was never the common denominator to all the disasters in his life and his failed relationships! To sum it up, he was a classic narcissist. As the months went by, I noticed how unhappy he was, and his toxic behavior was eating him inside. He always put on a fake happy disposition, but in reality, he was one of the unhappiest individuals I've ever met. Later I learned (from another neighbor) that he was smoking marijuana on a daily bases and drinking heavily.

My neighbor lying to himself was a tragedy to himself and others. I tried on many occasions to speak to him about his situation. During some of our conversations, he became very agitated. I could tell I was hitting a nerve that he never wanted to address. He was happy with his self-destructing state of mind. My message went in one ear and out the other. He never wanted to face reality because that reality would expose his false reality. If my neighbor had any care at all, he would have cared to fix himself and what he was doing wrong in his marriage and his family and with his friends. Instead, I fear he will wander through life as a narcissistic and lonely person.

Proverbs 3:15:   *"The righteous hates falsehood, but the wicked brings shame and disgrace."*

Proverbs bring this situation with my neighbor to heart. Understand yourself by being completely honest with yourself. Are you the 'Common Denominator?' Do you care enough to change to save your marriage, your family, and your friends? Understand what situation you are in by evaluating yourself. You can only be the best person when you become that person.

H: Asking yourself tough questions:

- Do you care enough?
- Does your family love you? Do you have a history of family neglect? Do you need counseling?
- Do you have friends who love you?
- Do you love yourself?
- Are you proud of your actions?
- Are others proud of you?
- How many people do you respect?
- Are you always seeking a new audience (friends)?
- How many people respect you?
- What are your priorities? Are your priorities selfish, or are they priorities of giving and nurturing your relationship?
- Most importantly, do you care enough to change yourself from hurting others?

To become the best partner in your marriage, you have to be honest with your partner and, most importantly, be honest with yourself.

There is only one way you become the person of your dreams and your partner's dreams. Seek after God. Join a Bible-based church that has men and women's bible studies, support groups for marriages, couples dating, family counseling, and other activities. Read the Bible every day. Listen to your favorite pastors on the radio while driving. Watch or listen to podcasts. Receive daily inspirational messages via email. Watch inspirational sermons on YouTube and other Internet platforms.

There are so many avenues to receive God's word and his loving support with today's technology. God has made it easier for Christians to strengthen and grow their faith.

With all the turmoil that the forces of darkness throw at us on a daily bases, we require a daily dose of Christian strength and wisdom.

4.10 Summary

1. How deep is your level of communication with your spouse?
2. Be a good listener and make a strong effort to understand your partner's point of view.
3. What level of communication are you at with your spouse? 'Surface, Mutual Sharing and 'All of Me.'
4. and All of Me.'
5. Non-verbal communication in marriage.
6. Words can create and destroy
7. Review the do's and don'ts in a marriage.
8. Don't say everything that comes to your mind, especially in an argument.
9. Being critical, fault-finding, and nagging is the death of a thousand cuts to a marriage.
10. Jealous and possessive characteristics in a partner will always ruin a relationship.
11. Lying erodes respect, honor, and loyalty in a relationship.
12. Does your family love you? Do you have a history of family neglect? Do you need counseling?
13. Seek after God to become the best person you've been created to be.

Notes:

Chapter 5: The Heart Of The Matter

Mathew 5:9: ESV *"Blessed are the peacemakers, for they shall be called sons of God."*

5.1 Peacemaker:

Are you a peacemaker in your marriage and life? Do you strive to keep harmony and love in your marriage and your daily walk?

Jesus points out in the Bible that it is not enough to just have peace; we also need to work on maintaining peace in our daily walk.

Do you always want to have it your way? Are you obsessed with winning and being always right? Being always right is not a good thing. Pick your battles and understand that your ego is pushing your obsession and eventual destruction in your relationships and yourself by always trying to be right.

I know a guy who has lost most of his relationships because of a mindset to win every battle, every argument, and even the small, petty battles. His blind and unfiltered obsession has pushed him to the point that he picks battles just to be in a fight. His mother and father are not on speaking terms with him, his friends will not speak to him, and sadly he is in the process of a divorce because he has bullied and driven his wife to a place of contempt and hatred. All because he has to win every battle and always be right! What a price to pay! Is it worth losing your friends, your family, and loved ones just to be right?

John 16:33: ESV *"I have said these things to you, that in me you may have peace. In the world, you will have tribulation. But take heart; I have overcome the world."*

"In the world, you will have tribulation." Jesus was saying that it would rain on everyone. The young, the old, the rich, the poor, the righteous, and the unrighteous, everyone will experience setbacks, hardships, betrayals, despair, enemies, and disappointments.

Do you lose your temper in traffic or bring the garbage you experienced at work home? It all starts with you and your daily attitude. We need to keep growing mentally, spiritually, and emotionally. You do not need to win every battle, but you do need to seek peace in your heart and soul.

I read that 80% of Americans did not buy or read a book last year. 33% of high school graduates will never read or pick up a book after graduation, and 42% of college graduates will not read another book after graduation. *

(Oct. 29, 2019 www.hogwartsprofessor.com)

These stats tell me that we as a nation are not growing mentally. What a shame on all the potential knowledge that could be obtained but is wasted. With learning, you become creative, experience success, and will achieve personal growth. B.B. King said it best; *"The beautiful thing about learning is that no one can take it away from you."*

Proverbs 1:7: ESV: *"The fear of the Lord is the beginning of knowledge; fools despise wisdom and instruction."*

And

Proverbs 18:15: ESV: *"An intelligent heart acquires knowledge, and the ear of the wise seeks knowledge."*

And

Proverbs 9:9: ESV: *"Give instruction to a wise man, and he will be still wiser, teach a righteous man, and he will increase in learning."*

5.2 Trust God

One of the most important things that we must learn is to **'Learn to trust God.'** To do this, we can open our Bible, listen to podcasts, listen to daily inspirational messages on the radio, television, or the Internet, and even receive daily emails of inspirational messages. If we do not currently read the Bible or receive God's daily word, we can start now to learn and understand how to trust God through His word and achieve inner peace. We can do this at home, in the car, or anywhere - it's never too late to search for God and make Him a part of our daily lives. It all begins with acknowledging and respecting that God has supernatural abilities. He created the universe, the science that keeps us all alive, and mankind itself. His love for us is abundant, and He loves us so much that He sacrificed His only son on the cross for our sins. When we repent, God forgives us of our sins, and He will never remember them.

Some people may believe that they have sinned to the point that God will never forgive them. This mindset is often caused by the demonic dark side, which wants people to believe they are lost without hope. However, this is far from the truth of God and His love. It is also insulting to God to believe that He will not forgive us. The same God who forgave all of the heroes in the Bible will surely forgive us of our sins.

In the Bible, there are many stories of how God forgave sinners who killed, had adultery affairs, cheated, and even turned their backs on God.

Moses: Killed a man and had severe anger issues.

Saul (Paul): Persecuted and killed Christians.

David: A Hero who killed Goliath but had an adultery affair and arranged the death of the husband with whom he was having an affair.

We all should use Joseph as one of the many examples given to us in the Bible by overcoming adversity and hardship and keeping God first. His brothers sold Joseph into slavery after his brothers almost killed him, his brothers lied to their father that wild animals killed Joseph, and worst of all, were delighted at the demise of Joseph's life. Yet all along, God loved Joseph and laid out a plan for him. Joseph endured hardship year after year, but Joseph never lost sight of God, and God never gave up on Joseph. In the end, when drought and famine ravaged the lands, his brothers were forced to seek food to avoid starvation. Joseph's brothers ventured to Egypt after hearing that the Egyptian government had an abundant food supply and was allocating food to non-Egyptians. Twenty-three years later, Joseph became second in charge of Egypt by miracles that only the hand of God could create. The brothers came before Joseph asking for food (not recognizing Joseph). Revenge in Joseph's heart could have thrown his brothers into slavery or even had them executed, but the integrity and mercy of Joseph teach us forgiveness, kindness, and love.

Joseph not only forgave his brothers, but he also fed them and had them bring their father back to Egypt to live with Joseph as one loving family in the Egyptian palace. The moral of the story about Joseph, even with the brother's evil work, God's love and forgiveness overruled darkness. We all should learn and meditate on Joseph's actions and God's love. It is important to understand what has happened to you in the past; if you have been hurt, betrayed, or experience abandonment, what Joseph overcame should inspire us all to seek God and understand that the meaning of Jesus and his scarifies on the cross. God loves us all and is waiting at the door for us to knock.

Luke 11: 9-10: *"So I say to you, ask, and it will be given to you; seek, and you will find; knock, and it will be opened to you. For everyone who asks, receives; and he who seeks, finds; and to him who knocks, it will be opened."*

God is always there for you! To have a faith-filled, happy, and abundant life, remember what God has said in **Luke 11: 9-10:** *"So I say to you, ask and it will be given to you."* God is speaking directly to us and saying, *"Ask me, and it is yours. "*

Ask God for peace in your heart, home, work, and every day and night. We have to keep seeking peace through God in order for us to grow in faith and love.

1 Peter 3:7: ESV: *"In the same way, you husbands must give honor to your wives. Treat your wife with understanding as you live together,"*

Seek Honor within yourself:

Have honor in your heart so you may have a long-lasting marriage. People ask me what the secret is to a long-lasting happy marriage. My answer is very simple, my wife and I enjoy each other's company by having God in our marriage, a joyous house, and honoring each other with love and peace.

The definition of '**Honor**' in Merriam-Webster dictionary is *'showing of usually merited respect.'*

How can we honor each other in marriage? In our marriage, I know my wife dreads the task of vacuuming. Ever since she was a little girl, my mother-in-law would tell me stories about her struggles trying to get my wife to vacuum. There are some things in life that we do not want to participate in. For my wife, it's playing with the vacuum. LOL…. For me, it is eating liver. (That's another story!).

So in respect and honor of my wife, I do all the vacuuming in the house. It's not my favorite thing to do, but I muster through it. Another way I honor and respect my wife is by picking up after myself. At first, this was a difficult habit for me to change. I used to come home and leave my clothes on the floor everywhere - in the bathroom, bedroom, and even the living room. I would watch TV, discard my sweatshirt, or remove my socks and leave them on the floor.

However, I eventually realized that my habits were a great irritation to my wife. I want nothing more than to make her happy, and she deserves to be happy. So, I made a concentrated effort to always place my clothes either in the laundry basket or hang them back up in the closet. I respect and honor my wife; her wishes are very important to me.

Keeping strife and argument out of your life and marriage is important. You have the power to control what is inside your life and what is around you. Too many of us allow the little irritation to bend us out of shape. For example, my wife always asking me to vacuum the house could irritate me. Instead, I choose to step back and understand that this is something my wife really does not like to do. So I take the initiative, pull the vacuum out, and do what needs to be done. It makes my wife happy, and there is peace and harmony in our house.

5.3 My Mother's Honor:

One of the greatest acts of honor and respect I have ever witnessed was from my mother toward my father. In late 1974, my father was diagnosed with lung cancer and had to have his left lung removed. Unfortunately, the cancer had already spread throughout his body, and the main growth was in his liver.

The doctors gave him a month to live and advised my mother to move him to a hospice. But being a direct and forward German lady, my mother refused to give up on her husband. She believed in the vows they took during their marriage, including "thru sickness and health," and insisted that no one could care for him better than she could. She vowed to take care of him until his last breath in his own bed.

My father was a quiet, hardworking man who enjoyed socializing after a few drinks. He was also a chain smoker, which he started during his time in the German army. He was a lieutenant in the German 6th Army (Wehrmacht), which was one of the leading forces in invade Russia and advance into Stalingrad. In February 1943, he was captured in Stalingrad, which is considered one of the bloodiest and deadliest battles of World War II. It is estimated that nearly two million people lost their lives in Stalingrad between August 1942 and February 1943. The Russian army did not favor or treat the German invaders of their country very well. Roughly 100,000 German troops were captured in Stalingrad and marched to Siberian POW camps. The march to the Siberian POW camps was better known as the; "The Road of Bones."

Most of the POWs died either from starvation or disease, on the 2-month march or in captivity. Out of the 100,000 German POWs, approximately 6,000 Germans survived.

I had asked my father on several occasions how he had survived all the harsh and brutal treatment from his Russian captors. He would give me answers in a roundabout way and always end with a German phrase, "Mann haste Mann" translated, "Man Hates Man."

He also said, "The prison guards' harsh treatment you would eventually get used to, but the Siberian winters you could never get used to." He told me that the winters were so cold to the extent that if you urinated into the air, the urine would freeze before it hit the ground.

My father told me a few short stories about the Russian prison guards and the daily beatings the German prisoners received. There were also stories of no food and the death from starvation of his fellow prisoners. He never elaborated on his stories. I know now that the trauma was too deep, even after thirty-five years, to get any details from him. Trauma torture and brutality are something war veterans never want to relive in their minds.

One story that my father told me in a little more detail than the other stories was a description of his POW camp. The camp had no fences, no barbwire, only the Siberian tundra that encircled the camp for hundreds and hundreds of miles. My father's living quarters were a dugout trench with wood and dirt for his roof. He would wear five layers of clothes and as many socks as his boots would fit over. As the months went on, he accumulated more layers of clothes. The clothes that he acquired saved his life. Unfortunately, the life-saving clothing was acquired from his fellow dead POWs. Hundreds of prisoners died each day, so there became an abundant amount of clothing to insulate the living POWs from the harsh sub-zero Siberian winter.

Escaping from his prisoner-of-war camp was never considered or even thought of. In my naive way, I asked him why he never tried to escape. He explained to me that no one could survive the Siberian wasteland. It was just a flat piece of ice with no shelter or food. The other reason is if you did make it to a small Russian village, the village people would hang you. The Germans were hated and never ever were shown any mercy by the villagers.

My father's first realization that the war had ended was when the Russian guards one day vanished. The guards just got up and left. Once a week, a train would pass near the POW camp. My father estimated it was several miles away. When there were no more guards, and the weather had improved, he and several other prisoners made their way to the train tracks, leaving behind thousands of prisoners that were near death and did not have the strength to make a journey battling through the Siberian elements.

Finding civilian clothes, my father was able to blend in with the Russian folk along with dozens of other prisoners. The ex-POWs were able to hitch a ride in an empty stock car that was used to haul cattle and other livestock through Russia.

I asked my father how he knew it was a cattle car, and he said because of the foot-deep manure on the floor.

For 20 days, my father jumped from one train to another, not knowing the direction the train would take him. On the 20th day, he arrived at the Russian - German border, the city of Berlin.

German POWs staging outside Leningrad City

"Road of Bones"

German POW's marching to Siberian Labor Camps

Some things stuck with my father from the war. My father was very passionate about me eating everything on my plate. Arguments would erupt with yelling and occasional disciplinary actions if I did not eat all the food on my plate. My mother would try to intervene and provide cover for me by saying he did not know or understand. She was talking about the starvation both of them faced during the war.

My mother's house was bombed when she was a young teenager living in Wiesbaden, Germany. My father experienced starvation while he was in the Russian POW camp with no food, only his dead comrades as the only supplement food source. My mother and my grandmother would search for food at the garbage dumps and other German military trash sites. Relief came towards the end of the war when the American military occupied her city. Food became a little more available because the American Army and Air Force would distribute food such as potatoes, bread, and even military MREs (Meals, Ready to Eat) to the German civilians.

In 1953 my parents met; I believe it was in the town of Wiesbaden where my mother was raised. After a brief courtship, my parents married. My father first moved to Northern Nevada with his sister and worked as a hotel cook, and was saving money for my mother to come to America. While my mother stayed in Germany, she helped take care of her mother and rebuild the family lace manufacturing business.

My fathers' sister married a man that owned a hotel called the Minden Inn in Nevada near the California border. My father began his career as a cook at the hotel and became passionate about the culinary arts. In 1955 my mother moved to America. My parents worked hard to be a part of the American dream.

I understand now the tough life my parents experienced and what horrors they must have survived. I did not see much of my father because he worked 10 to 12 hours seven days a week. My father and I did not have the best father-son relationship because he ruled the house in a military fashion. As I have aged in years, I now realize he was the hardest-working man I have known. At the time, being young and foolish, I could not see my father expressing his love through his hard work and long hours. He worked hard to put a roof over our heads and food on the table. I am grateful for all the sacrifices my father and mother made for me. Like most adult children, I wish I could go back in time and tell them how much I love them and how deeply appreciative I am.

My father was not a religious man, and my mother would attend church occasionally. I know God had his hedge of protection on my parent's life. I learned from my parents that anyone can endure life's extreme hardships, from life-threatening turmoil and severe despair. You can, and you will endure, my mother and father would say to each other.

We all receive wounds, some deeper than others, but always remember that wounds heal with time, prayer, and belief in God for your healing.

Ephesians 4:2-3: *"With all humility and gentleness, with patience, bearing with one another in love, eager to maintain the unity of the Spirit in the bond of peace."*

Toward the end of my father's life, he was bedridden. The cancer had dwindled a strong 6'3" man who weighed 225 pounds down to a frail 85 pounds. I witnessed my mother wash my father in bed, feed him in bed, read to him in bed, and with love, commitment, and devotion, she would also change his diapers. My mother was an inspiration to me by showing through actions what honor, respect, loyalty, commitment, and love is.

My father passed away from cancer in 1977 to be with God. Because of my mother's love and compassion, he lived 3 months longer than what the doctors told us.

My witness of my mother's actions and their love for each other is a testimony of love, honor, and spousal loyalty and commitment. Through sickness and health and richer or poorer, their commitment to each other showed me what God's design is for marriage.

1 Peter 3:1-2: *"Likewise, wives, be subject to your own husbands, so that even if some do not obey the word, they may be won without a word by the conduct of their wives, when they see your respectful and pure conduct."*

5.4 Summary

1. Are you the peacemaker in your relationship?
2. Understand that it will rain on everyone.
3. Learn to 'Trust God.'
4. Honor each other in marriage.
5. Are you committed to your spouse?

Notes:

Chapter 6: The Family

Psalm 127: 3-5 ESV *"Behold, children are a heritage from the Lord, the fruit of the womb a reward. Like arrows in the hand of a warrior are the children of one's youth. Blessed is the man who fills his quiver with them! He shall not be put to shame when he speaks with his enemies in the gate."*

6.1 My Early Years

I was born an only child with no brothers or sisters. For the longest time, I believed the saying was "lonely child" instead of "only child." I always yearned for a brother or sister and prayed that someday I could call anyone my own sibling. The neighborhood kids all had siblings, and I admired the inseparable bond they shared. Yes, they fought with each other, but if one of the neighbored kids got in a jam, their sibling was there to back them up. As the old saying goes, "You mess with me, you mess with my family." Someone always had his or her back!

I believe one of the driving forces behind my interest in athletics was that I had no one my age to hang out with. My world growing up was mostly with adults. I had my parents, a couple of aunts, and two-second cousins who were 25 years older than me. You could say I had a very small family. Additionally, my father ran the household like a military boot camp. I had to make my bed, finish all my meals, and do countless chores. Playing with the neighborhood kids was discouraged and frowned upon. My parents would tell me that playing outside with other children was not practical or useful, and if I wanted to be outside, I should mow the lawn or pick weeds.

I understand now what my parents were all about. Growing up as a child and a teenager in Germany during World War Two and serving in the Hitler Youth when you were ten years of age did not allow much playtime. You grew up fast. Most children in Germany during the 1940s had no childhood. Their youth was bypassed directly into adulthood. The German culture at the time was a strict regimen of survival, training, and focusing on serving the Nazi government.

At around 12 years of age, I started playing sports for school teams and staying after school. Every day I played in the gym or playground, either basketball, flag football, handball, or anything to keep me from going home. We would play until the janitor or some school official would tell us to leave because the lights were being turned off or they would be locking the gates.

I knew right at the start, when playing sports with others that some guys had more talent than me. What could I do about it? I concluded to practice and practice and even practice some more.

During my freshman year in High School, one of the coaches approached me and asked if I had ever played volleyball. I had no idea that volleyball was a varsity sport. In truth, I did not even know what volleyball was. If it meant I could stay after school and run around, I was all in. I was not the best volleyball player, but I could jump, and I had God-given height. I practiced and practiced hitting the ball against the wall, bump passing against a wall, and even working on my serve against a wall. My parents did not appreciate all my practicing against a wall because the wall I chose was the garage door to our home. My parents had to replace the garage door after six months because of all the dents in the thin aluminum surface of the door. Opppssss, my bad... I refocused my wall practice in the gym or outside at the school's handball courts.

6.2 The Family Plan

Ephesians 1:11 *"Through our union with Christ, we too have been claimed by God as his own inheritance. Before we were even born, he gave us our destiny, that we would fulfill the plan of God who always accomplishes every purpose and plan in his heart."*

God has a destiny for everyone … Listen and obey, and you will come into your destiny. Because Coach Hubbard approached me and asked me to play on the high school volleyball team, I was able to go to college. Not just any college but one of the most prestigious Christian Universities on the planet.

Pepperdine University was a dream come true. I would have never attended college if it was not for volleyball. God laid out a plan for my education and my Christian life. I was able to attend Pepperdine on a full-ride athletic scholarship. The only thing I was responsible for was paying for my books. What a blessing God had graced me with! Through volleyball, I met some of my lifelong friends and built a work ethic of being diligent and responsible.

Being a division one-student athlete made me grow into a responsible man. But more importantly, the Christian atmosphere and education that Pepperdine offered helped me understand and respect the bible, Jesus, and God.

Several years after graduating, God had another plan for my life. I started considering taking a real estate course and getting my sales license. There was a real estate class being offered on one of the auxiliary classes near the UCLA Westwood campus. It just so happened that my future wife was also attending that same class.

God had arranged our meeting during one of the class mid-session breaks. What are the chances that my schedule and the timing of our meeting happened? I was living in Manhattan Beach at the time, an easy 45-minute drive to the UCLA campus. I could have just attended one of the many real estate classes offered near me in the South Bay. The real estate class in Westwood somehow stood out, and I signed up and attended.

My wife, Claudette, and I married in 1985. I knew she was the one because she was everything I had been looking for. Claudette was a dream come true; she was smart, absolutely gorgeous, she was always happy, never stopped smiling, and positive. She was the no-drama type of person, kind, but most importantly, she had one of the largest Christian hearts I had ever met in a person. It was a no-brainer to marry Claudette. There is one item that I forgot to mention, Claudette had a huge family, I mean huge.... Three brothers, two sisters, twenty-something cousins, and many aunts, uncles, and other immediate relatives. I describe her family as a tribe. I knew in the back of my mind that I was going to marry someone with a large family. Once again, God came through for me. Thank you, Jesus.

In 1986 we had our first child. Wow, what a miracle childbirth is... I remember holding my son in the delivery room, just sobbing and thanking god for the miracle I held in my arms. I had never held a baby before, and I was in awe of how beautiful and perfect he was.

Never being around babies or other young children, I had no clue what child rearing was. We brought Chasen home, and on the first day, I realized I was absolutely clueless about being a father. The first evening with my family in our little apartment was terrifying. All these thoughts came into my mind on providing for my son and wife; what about health insurance? How secure was my job? What happens if I lose my job? What then? If I lose my job, how will I provide for them? On and on, the forces of evil came bombarding me with negative thoughts.

I remember that I got down on my knees after a week of having these negative and frightening thoughts and asking God for direction and blessing and to protect my family with security. A small whispering voice inside of me said, "I've got you ... you have not come all this way to fail. I love you, and I love your family."

1 John 5:18: *"We know that everyone who has been born of God does not keep on sinning, but he who was born of God protects him, and the evil one does not touch him."*

Looking back to those early days, I can thank God over and over again for the path he set in front of me. For his daily protection, guidance, favor, and, most important, his unwavering love.

If you are a young couple just starting out with small children, my best advice is to pray every day and ask God to bless your family and your children and seek his direction for you and your family. God is a loving God who is there for you and your family. Strengthen your spiritual growth by joining a Bible-based church and listening to faith-filled music. Receive God's word through the radio, podcast, or emails daily.

The world is becoming more and more chaotic and darker with porn, violence, adultery, Hollywood's exposure of its immoral doctrine, education system, and its sexual message to young children, including government corruption and manipulation. We need to receive a daily dose (sometimes three or four doses a day) of spiritual inspiration to keep our minds and soul focused on God's direction.

Having your children learn at an early age the love of God and the scarifies and teachings of Jesus is one of the most rewarding gifts a mother and father can give. Providing spiritual salvation to your children will be a reward to you not only in heaven but here on earth, and spiritual salvation is the greatest gift you can give your children.

Proverbs 22:6 ESV *"Train up a child in the way he should go; even when he is old, he will not depart from it."*

By teaching the word of God, you will plant the seed of love, honor, respect, morals, values, humility, and self-worth in your children. There is no greater gift a parent can give their child than the teaching of the spirit of God.

6.3 Raising Children

We all have regrets about how we raised our children. I especially regret the harsh disciplinary actions I took as a parent. In raising my son, I drew on my own childhood experiences from my father. I look back and realize there were so many other choices I could have made raising my son, and to this day, I have great remorse for my actions. I was a hard, no-nonsense father. If my son did not do as asked, then he was sent to the corner or even spanked. I know now that parents should never raise their hand to their children. There are so many alternatives to discipline than spanking.

I am so proud of my son and the adult he has become. My son is so caring, loving, and smart. It makes me so proud to call him "Son." I thank God for the gift of my son. And now he is a father who is absolutely becoming one of the best dads in the world. My son is a true blessing to my wife, our beautiful granddaughter, Sahara, and me.

Young parents need to realize that children require structure when being raised. They long for boundaries in their lives. And yes, they will push to see where those boundaries are and see if they can expand those established parental boundaries.

My sister-in-law is a schoolteacher and has raised three

amazing children. One of her notable parenting techniques is using the "cause and effect rule" - if you do this, then this will be the outcome. This approach works in both positive and negative ways. Her children are encouraged to make a conscious effort towards positive actions daily, whether it's completing homework, participating in team sports, or making choices in their everyday lives. If their actions result in negative consequences, she implements disciplinary actions such as being grounded, losing television privileges, doing extra dish duty, or being denied dessert while their siblings receive theirs. Although it may seem harsh, it is an effective method. Conversely, she and her husband also reward their children with gifts when they make positive choices or achieve success. They may go on ice cream trips or shopping for clothes when their children bring home good grades or complete chores without being asked.

My wife and I have always wanted another child. In 1990 God gave us our beautiful daughter. I thought the feeling of complete joy in the delivery room was a one-time occurrence. No way... when I held my little baby girl, I sobbed like the first time when I held my newborn son. The miracle of life is the most amazing gift God does right in front of our own eyes. We are all God's creation, and to be there in person and witness life being born is the most amazing event ever. Words cannot describe the miracle of birth.

We are so proud of our children and the great individuals they have become. It is really an honor to call my children "my son and my daughter."

Every parent wishes that their children surpass them in financial growth, education, intelligence, and even spiritual growth. My son is a lawyer, and my daughter has achieved her MBA. They are smart, funny, engaging, loving, and most of all, God-fearing. What a blessing they are in our lives.

As adult children, they have become our best friends. Parents can transition into friendship with their children once the children have reached adult age. Not at 18, but maybe at 25 years of age or later. Some adult children mature even later in life.

Some parents make the mistake of trying to be their children's friend when the child is young or even a teenager. I have seen many of our friends make that mistake in attempting to be their child's pal. Big, big mistake! Children, especially at a young age, require structure and boundaries. Parents' role is to be exactly that, "Parents." Not best of buds or best of friends. Parents need to guide and mentor their children. Best friends do not mentor and do not give guidance or even discipline to their friends.

God made you a parent, not a friend or buddy to your child. When my daughter was around twelve, she became an amazing tennis player. She started competing at the national level and doing very well. I started coaching her tennis when she was five on our community tennis courts. By the age of twelve, I felt our father-daughter relationship becoming strained. I was playing several roles with my daughter, being the parent and her tennis coach. You can't become both! I saw so many parents with older children in the tennis world having horrible, deteriorating relationships with their teenage tennis children. I did not want that to happen to my daughter and me. I valued our relationship too much for our relationship to be soured because I took on another role other than being her loving father. The remedy was to have her coached by someone else. I fell back into being the parent and gave up the coaching responsibilities. Sometimes I would give my unprofessional tennis opinion, and most of the time, my daughter reminded me that I was not the coach. Lol …

It is such a joy to have a strong relationship with your children. And now that our son and daughter are older and have children of their own, it makes it even more special. Both my children are amazing parents themselves. They must have received that from their wonderful mother.

I cannot emphasize enough that parents must realize their role in their children's lives. Parents are not meant to be their children's friends or buddies and not their child's coaches.

It's impossible to be a disciplinarian if you are your child's friend. Wait until your children grow up and become functioning adults before you become best of buddies.

Cassidy and Chasen

6.4 Family Balance

Ecclesiastes 3:1-8 ESV: *"For everything, there is a season and a time for every matter under heaven; a time to be born, and a time to die, a time to plant, and a time to pluck up what is planted; a time to kill, and a time to heal; a time to break down, and a time to build up; a time to weep, and a time to laugh; a time to mourn, and a time to dance; a time to cast away stones, and a time to gather stones together; a time to embrace, and a* *time to refrain from embracing."*

Balancing time with spouse, family, work, hobbies, friends, and God can be very exhausting and even demoralizing. Neglecting one area while focusing too much on another is not fulfilling or balanced.

Early in my marriage, I realized it was no longer solely about me; I had a teammate. To make our marriage work as a team, I had to be conscious of my wife's needs, wants, and desires. Likewise, my wife became understanding of my desires and wants.

This was the beginning of our new life together, and we had to learn the fine details of balancing our responsibilities and commitments.

I'm not suggesting that you lose yourself completely in your spouse. However, it's essential to understand that your spouse is now a part of your life and needs to be involved. Share your interests and your world, whether it's sports, books, travel, cooking, cars, animals, building things, or even your unconventional taste in movies. It's okay if your spouse doesn't enjoy everything that you do. Your spouse will have their own hobbies and interests that bring them joy. It's essential to have your own personal hobbies and things that make you happy. However, always remember not to become entirely consumed with your own happiness. Make sure that your teammate is involved in decision-making, planning, and your world. I find that I'm in a happy place when I can share my events and experiences with my wife.

Most importantly, I make an effort to see if she would be interested in what I'm doing or interested in. A good example of this is when my wife and I started playing Pickle Ball together. I've always been a tennis player and looked down on Pickle Ball as a lesser sport. So one day, I finally agreed to go play with her. On the first day, we had so much fun playing together and also playing against each other. We laughed during and after playing the game. When we finished playing (after 2 hours) Pickle Ball, we shared and talked about the highlights of our matches. Four years later, my wife and I still play Pickle Ball together and against each other and are still having a blast sharing and reminiscing about our games. We are also making dozens of new friends through Pickle Ball.

It is important to keep sports lighthearted and not too competitive. Playing on the same team, such as Pickle Ball, Tennis, or even Softball teams, can be stressful in a marriage if one of the partners (usually the man) is very competitive and places everything on winning. Remember, it is only a game that you and your spouse are to enjoy; you are not playing for a multi-million-dollar shoe contract. Have fun and relish the moment and enjoy each other's company. You are building memories and stories; make your experience a happy and long-lasting one.

When I became a husband, God taught me to love, cherish and honor my wife by self-sacrifice, some of the things I really enjoyed during my single life. For example, I used to work out for two to three hours daily, mostly in the evening. I would also go surfing early every morning (if there were waves) - not to mention my job from 9 to 5, Monday thru Friday. There was not much room for dating or even having a wife, but I fell in love with the most amazing woman I have ever met. To keep my marriage healthy, I needed to change and give up my old routine and build a new routine that included my wife and, later to include my children.

Things to do with your partner:

1. Workout as a Couple

One of the healthiest and most fun ways to spend more time together as a couple is to become a 'Workout Couple' in a gym.

Studies show that if you have a workout partner, you will and are more likely to stay with the exercise routine. Not only will you be more committed, but you will also work out harder and longer rather than working out alone.

Another fun workout routine is riding bikes. There are dozens of trails (or just ride your bike in the neighborhood) and parks to ride and explore. Not only are you and your partner outdoors, breathing fresh air, but you are also getting great aerobic exercise.

Try couples yoga. One of the most beneficial forms of exercise is yoga which creates flexibility, strength, and inner peace.

Hit the water with kayaks, stand-up paddle boards, or canoes. These paddle activities are fun and can be very adventurous. They provide a complete day of activities, burn calories and create fun and memorable experiences.

Another fun and bonding couple exercise is racket sports such as pickle ball, tennis, racquetball, and other court sports. Public parks offer free court time, so you do not have to join an expensive club.

The pickleball community is growing; many community centers offer free introductory courses. Also, most community centers provide you with a paddle and ball to practice with.

2. Shop together / Cook meals together

It is delightful to go shopping with your significant other, pick out ingredients, and find the perfect bottle of wine to complement the dish you plan to create in the kitchen.

My wife and I enjoy cooking together, and shopping for high-quality ingredients is an important part of the experience. We love seeking out fresh, exotic ingredients that will make our meals even better than the last.

Of course, part of the fun of shopping for ingredients is finding the right wine to pair with our dish. While we're not sommeliers, the Vivino Wine App has been an incredible tool for us. It provides ratings and pairing suggestions, as well as information on the regions the grapes come from and pricing. We always look forward to our romantic date nights at home, where we can enjoy our home-cooked meals and perfectly paired wines.

3. Schedule a date night on a regular basis

Scheduling a date night with your significant other on a regular basis can be a great way to reduce stress in your relationship and spend quality time together. Whether you choose to do it once a week or once a month, getting away from the house and all the responsibilities that come with it - cooking, cleaning, childcare - can do wonders for your relationship.

Taking the time to get out and do something fun together can improve communication, reduce feelings of boredom, and create opportunities for intimacy. In fact, research suggests that regular date nights can even help lower the divorce rate! So, make it a priority to schedule a date night with your partner and commit to making it happen. Whether you go out for a nice dinner, take a walk in the park, or try a new activity together, the important thing is that you're taking time to focus on each other and strengthen your connection.

Dating Ideas:

Dinner and a movie: Just like when you started dating, go out and have a romantic dinner followed up by a movie. An alternative is to stay home and order pizza and snuggle on the couch with a good glass of wine. Snuggling on the couch with pizza and wine, what else could you want?

Alternatives to movies: If you feel more extravagant, there are alternatives to movies. How about attending concerts, going to live theater and sports events? Nothing like rooting for your favorite home team.

Double date: It is lots of fun double dating with your best friends. There is a unique experience every time my wife and I double date with good friends. Memories are shared, and new memories are created.

Plan a weekend getaway: Traveling with your significant other is always a great way to enjoy each other's company. Destinations planning to a tropical paradise or an exciting location like an Air B.B. in the mountains. If you are more into the physical / active vacation, book a reservation at a sports camp for tennis, pickle ball, or waterskiing resort. Whatever you choose, when it comes to vacation getaways, the Internet provides limitless opportunities.

Adventure to a new restaurant: Create a goal and explore every exotic restaurant in your neighborhood, such as Indian, Thai, and even Mexican locations. Get out and explore new locals; it's fun exploring and sharing new adventures with your partner.

Head to the theme park: Spend a day at the zoo or museum. My wife and I like to explore new exhibits when they hit town at our local downtown museum. It's fun and interesting, and it's always enlightening that we both want to keep learning about new stuff.

John 15:1-27: *"I am the true vine, and my Father is the vinedresser. Every branch in me that does not bear fruit he takes away, and every branch that does bear fruit he prunes that it may bear more fruit. Already you are clean because of the word that I have spoken to you. Abide in me, and I in you. As the branch cannot bear fruit by itself unless it abides in the vine, neither can you unless you abide in me. I am the vine; you are the branches. Whoever abides in me and I in him, he it is that bears much fruit,* *for apart from me, you can do nothing.*"

Things You Can Do As a Family:

Enjoying and building memories with your wife and children are some of the most precious times we can experience. Creating family memories helps build the family core. In today's busy world, family time is essential for children because they do not get the required attention that is needed and spiritual foundation.

Our children always cherished having dinner together as a family. We still share stories on events that took place at the dinner table 25 years ago. Dinnertime was a time to share the day's events. It's a time to discuss school experiences, tell jokes, and share what happens during the day. And most importantly, it was a time for us all to bow our heads and thank Jesus for our food, the love we shared, and his blessing.

Here are some activities you can experience as a family.

Attend church as a family: The Book of John provides direct guidance by emphasizing that we, as a family, are part of the vine. By participating in church and its events together, we strengthen the holy vine that ties us and nourishes us with spiritual nutrients. Praying together is another powerful way to strengthen our family bond.

The words of **Joshua 24:15** resonate with us: **"As for me and my household, we will serve the Lord."** This commitment to serving God as a family is a powerful way to unite us and provide a sense of purpose and direction. Participating in church activities and praying together as a family can provide comfort and support during challenging times and deepen our relationships with each other and God. By investing in our family's spiritual health, we can create a strong foundation for our relationships and our lives.

Go Camping: Exploring and sleeping out under the stars is fun and helps build unity. All the mini experiences that roll into camping, such as fishing, hiking, and exploring, build great family bonding experiences.

Have family picnics: Picnics are like a one-day camping excursion. You can do all the things like camping in one day. Picnics are a great way to see how the family enjoys the outdoors. If the picnic is a tremendous success, then camping is in your future.

What to do on those rainy days? Board games are a great way to have a family fun day on rainy and snowy days. Some games that made us all laugh were 'Twister' and the board game 'Monopoly.' There are also dozens of card games that can be played and learned.

What to do on those snowy days? Build a giant snowman. Go for the record and build a snowman larger than last year's snowman. Have a snowman-building contest or even a snowman fashion show. If it's too cold outside, build a puzzle as a family.

Family vacations: Take to the road and explore interesting destinations. Take in destinations that the children are learning in school, such as Civil War locations and take a trip to Washington D.C. and see all the historical sights.

Family bike rides: Head to one of the many trails located in parks and or around your neighborhood. Riding bikes as a family is a fun way to explore new areas. Don't forget to wear a helmet.

Miniature Golf: Great time to spend half of the day showing off your mini-golf skills. Team up as parents against the children for laughs and good times.

Head to the beach or the lake: As a family, we would always head to the beach on those nice sunny weekends. There is so much to do along the shore, such as building sandcastles, playing with the Frisbee, flying a kite, or just having fun playing in the shallow water.

Play hide and seek: You can play hide and seek indoors or outdoors.

And don't forget all the church activities that are offered at your local Bible-based churches: The best way to find church activities is to go online and search what activities interest you and your family. Or call and speak to the church program direct for more personal questions.

6.5 Summary

1. Know that God has a destiny for everyone.
2. Recognize what God has placed in your life and appreciate God's Blessings.
3. Receive spiritual inspiration daily.
4. God placed children in your life to be their parents.
5. Understand your priorities when it comes to your family.
6. Enjoy each other's company.
7. Build memories with family activities.

Notes:

Conclusion

**"A good marriage would be between a blind wife
and a deaf husband":**

Quote from Michel de Montaigne

Before moving forward into a serious relationship, it is important to understand yourself first to figure out what makes you happy and what makes you unhappy and annoyed. This can be a hard task for many since many of us do not like to see the reality of ourselves. However, if you are not content with yourself and don't love yourself, how can you expect a happy and meaningful relationship with someone else?

One common mistake that I see individuals make is comparing themselves to others. "My neighbor has a nice car. My neighbor is funny and fun. My neighbor has a great personality, my neighbor has great hair, and my neighbor is so successful. We keep on comparing ourselves to others.... STOP comparing yourself to others right now, and know that God made you a perfect person in his eyes.

You are a child of the most powerful. You have royal spiritual DNA, be proud of that and appreciate the breath God gave you. We are all sinners, but God's glory, forgiveness, and love for us are endless.

If you feel that you are lacking in anything, then change it.... If you feel overweight, work out and change your eating habits. If you feel you are underdeveloped in education, take courses online or return to school.

Do a critical analysis of who you are and examine any negative traits you may possess, then work on changing them. Are you a gossiper? Are you negative all the time? Are you a narcissist (everything is about you)? Are you conceded? Are you selfish? The list goes on and on. Commit to changing them through prayer and effort. To have a successful and fulfilling marriage, you must contribute joy, happiness, love, and commitment.

Over the years, I've come across reports and headlines concerning the divorce rate. Recently I've noticed the mainstream media harping on Christian and non-Christian marriages. The debate is about Christian marriages lasting longer than non-Christian marriages.

The statistics show a strong connection between Christian marriages and the success rate versus non-Christian marriages with higher divorce rates when compared to the United States population.

Unfortunately, in the United States, since 1970, church attendance has been declining, and individuals that identify as Christians have been declining. Thus marriages have shown a dramatic decline for both Christians and non-Christians. In the past 50 years, America has had the highest divorce rate among Western nations.

God created a covenant with the Hebrews to be faithful to Israel in the Old Testament. From the Hebrews, early Christians also adopted faith in God's marriage covenant. Christian couples, in marriage, vow to live in the future as one not just by emotion (love, infatuation, passion) but to be devoted and loyal to each other, with God's covenant at the center of their marriage. The choice to live in the future with God's covenant at the center of marriage will strengthen and bond relationships for all the years we are on this earth.

To base your marriage on the present moment is setting your

relationship on 'Hollywood's' hollow definition of romance, sex, and "what can you do for me now" culture. Without God's marriage covenant, most (a very high percentage, 43%) couples are doomed and get divorced within eight years. Also, the average age for divorce in America is between 25 and 39.

The most common and very serious reason for divorce is spousal abuse. Abuse can be in the form of physical and mental. Any person experiencing abuse in their relationship should seek immediate help and counseling. Law enforcement agencies should be contacted immediately if a spouse's life is endangered. Some marriages are not lucky to get help when abused in the relationship. The safety of the spouse and the children should always be the priority. Reasons for divorce may also include; marital infidelity, financial hardship, lack of intimacy, weight gain, selfish partner, addiction, poor communication, narcissism, and losing respect.

The decline of Christians is a direct coloration to the decline of couples' Likelihood of Marriage.' for both the black and white communities. The bar graph on the next pages shows that marriage in the United States is rapidly declining.

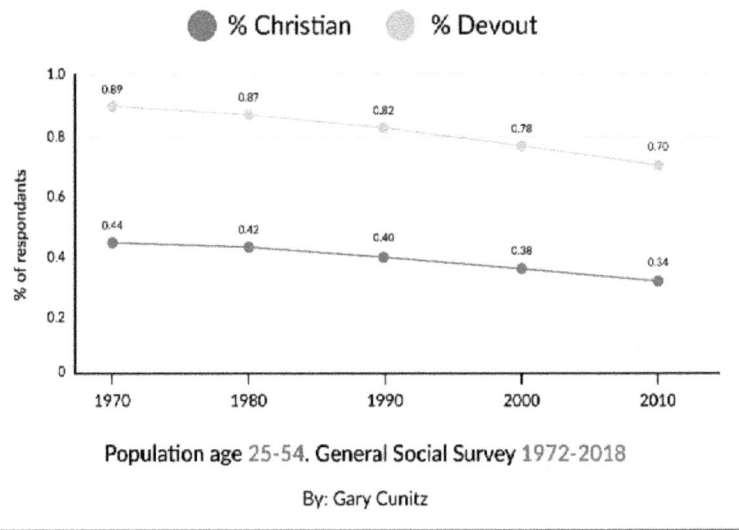

Percent Identifying as Christian and Attending Church Regularly

● % Christian   ◌ % Devout

Population age 25-54. General Social Survey 1972-2018

By: Gary Cunitz

*Institute for Family Studies, March 4th, 2020, By Brian Hollar/Graph by: Gary Cunitz

*National Survey of Family Growth from 1995 to 2019

Devout Christians attend Church two to three times a month: Yellow line.

Persons identify as Christian (not practicing) declined in the United States: Blue Line

Ages 25-54

Internet search: General Christian marriage statistics, Christian marriages, Christian divorces

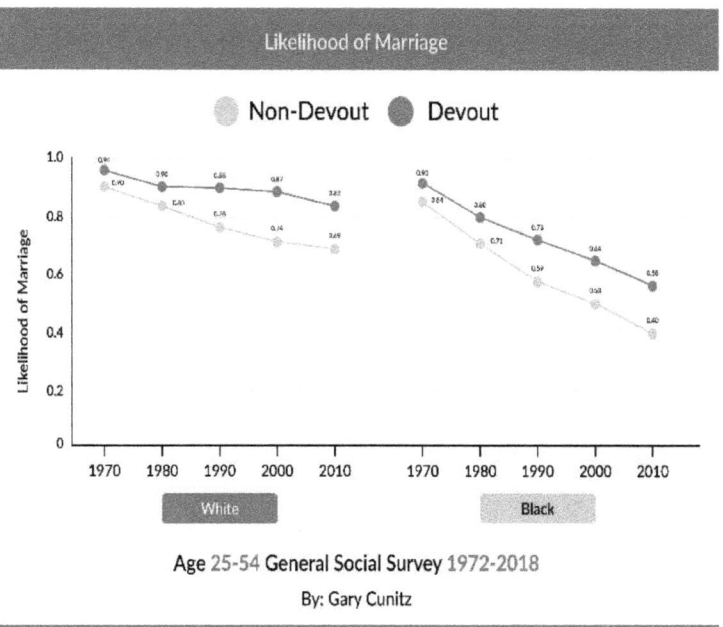

Age 25-54 General Social Survey 1972-2018

By: Gary Cunitz

Institute for Family Studies, March 4th, 2020, by Brian Hollar/Graph by: Gary Cunitz

*Life Studies .org

*US Bureau of Labor Statistics, Oct. 2013, June 2018.

Individuals identify as just Christians, non-practicing: Yellow line

Devout Christians attend Church two to three times a month: Blue line

Two racial segments of the United States: White Population and Black Population

Ages 25-54

Internet search: General Christian marriage statistics, Christian marriages, Christian divorces, Black vs. White marriages

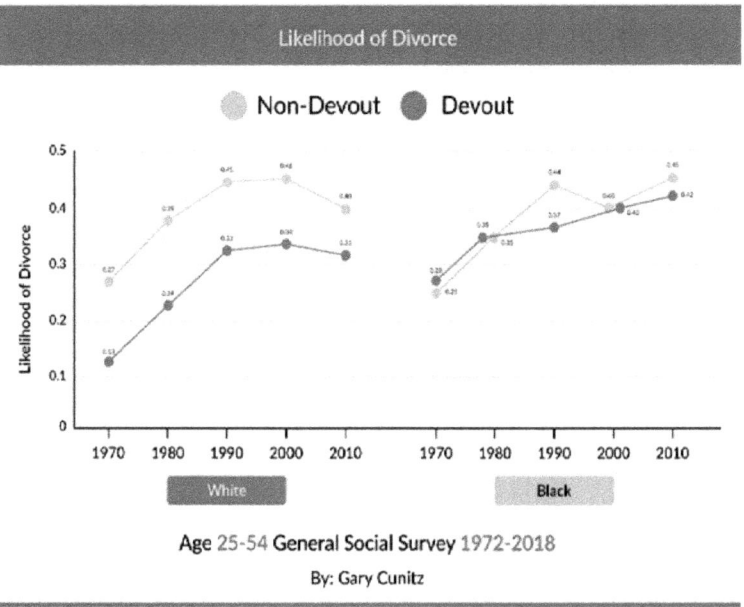

Likelihood of Divorce

Age 25-54 General Social Survey 1972-2018
By: Gary Cunitz

The 'Likelihood of Divorce' is increasing in the United States for both non-practicing and devout Christians.

*Institute for Family Studies, March 4th, 2020, By Brian Hollar/Graph by: Gary Cunitz

Devout Christians attend Church two to three times a month: Blue Line. Not practicing Christians: Yellow line.

Two racial segments of the United States: White Population and Black Population.

Age 25-54. General Social Survey 1972 – 2018

Internet search: General Christian marriage statistics, Christian marriages, Christian divorces, Black vs. White divorces.

After studying and reading many articles on religion's impact on an individual and marriages, I've become more convinced that Christians are one of the strong fibers that hold our society together. There is significant stability and instability between

Christians and non-Christians regarding marriage.

My Take-Away

Christians of any age, male or female, at all income levels averaged a higher level of commitment to their marital partners with greater satisfaction on being married. It was also noted that Christians had lower divorce rates than non-Christians because of values, morals, and respect for being married.

In the book of Genesis, God's creation and design of marriage were perfect. Adam was created first, and Eve was created to be Adam's partner in marriage for eternity.

Genesis 2:21-22: *"So the LORD God caused the man to fall into a deep sleep; and while he was sleeping, he took one of the man's ribs and closed up the place with flesh. Then the LORD God made a woman from the rib he had taken out of the man, and he brought her to the man."*

Genesis 2:23-24: *"The man said, This is now bone of my bones and flesh of my flesh; she shall be called woman, for she was taken out of man." "For this reason, a man will leave his father and mother and be united with his wife, and they will become one flesh."*

In honoring marriage, you are honoring God. God designed marriage to be joyous and successful. We must place God between the husband and wife for a happy and long-lasting marriage. The closer each partner draws to God, the stronger the marriage becomes.

Therefore if a Christian marries a non-Christian, it is easy to speculate that the marriage's failure is more likely than two like-minded Christians marrying. This is just a general observation based on statistical facts. So-called Christians who say they belong to a church have little faith in a successful marriage. True believing

Christians involved in their faith by submitting themselves to God actively learn scripture and surround themselves with their spouse and children with God-fearing friends and family. They take marriage more seriously and are more devoted to the marriage body. Faith in our Living God is essential for the success of a marriage.

If your marriage is on the rocks, do not look at your partner and blame them. Start with yourself and ask Jesus for strength. Jesus says in **John 15:5:** *"Apart from me, you can do nothing."* And **1 Peter 5:5:** says, *"God opposes the proud but gives grace to the humble."* Are you a humble servant? Are you humble to your partner?

The opposite of humility is pride. Merriam-Webster Dictionary defines pride as: 'Too high of an opinion of one's self, ability or worth. A feeling of being better than others.'

Pride leads to marital conflict and, in some cases, irreparable damage. Best described in **2 Corinthians 3:14:** *"But their minds were hardened."*

What pride does is it closes the mind and develops selfishness, stubbornness, arrogance, vanity, conceitedness, self-importance, judgment, and self-loathing. It is difficult for any marriage to survive if either spouse possesses these traits.

Understanding selfishness can only start when you recognize your prideful actions. Then you can start on the road of personal repair. Paul wrote an amazing scripture that directly addresses the prideful mindset in **Philippians 2-3:** *"Do nothing out of selfish ambition or vain conceit. Rather, in humility, value others before yourselves."*

Value yourself last; your wife, children, friends, and family should always come before you. Once you accept and be the person who washes others' feet, you are on the path of humility and redemption.

A Prayer to get you started on the road to healing:

"Heavenly Father, I come before you knowing that you will change me and dissolve the chains of my prideful actions. I appreciate the strength you gave me by making me walk in humility, allowing me to understand that I will place others before myself."

"Heavenly Father, thank you for the gifts and blessings you have given me."

"For the Kingdom and the glory of God will reign forever and ever, in Christ, we pray." Amen.

Biblical Verses

I've listed all the biblical verses by sections I used in this book with an added personal insight. The spirit guides us in mysterious ways. Reading bible verses helps us to understand God's word and his teachings. The New Testament brings us closer to understanding Jesus Christ as a man and the Son of God.

I hope the following verses help you walk with Christ, and I pray that these verses aid you and your partner in strengthening your relationship, your marriage and your family.

Power of Prayer and the Power of Jesus Christ:

John 3:16: *"For God so loved the world, that he gave his only Son, that whoever believes in him should not perish but have eternal light."*

Believe in Jesus, and you will be rewarded with eternal life in heaven. John 3:16 makes it so easy to understand the mercy and forgiveness God has promised us to receive his salvation. I've heard it said that it would be an insult to our Heavenly Father if we discarded the death of Jesus and his resurrection. Jesus did not die and be raised on the third day to be dismissed. Jesus died on the cross for our salvation and us. We should honor and always respect God because he so loved the world that he gave his only son to be tormented and crucified.

Romans 12:12: *"Be joyful in hope, patient in affliction, and faithful in prayer."*

As we reach our marriage age, some of us get anxious, and in our nature, we try to excel in choosing the right companion. Romans 12:12 tells us to wait and be patient. God has someone for you, don't rush into a marriage and regret it because you were not patient. "Be joyful in hope?" tells us why we should wake up and thank God every morning for the beautiful day before us and be joyful that this might be the day that special someone comes into our lives.

Relationships, Personal Growth, and Strengthening the Marriage:

Proverbs 20:3: "It is an honor for a man to avoid strife, but every fool will be quarreling."

Happiness in a relationship, especially in a marriage, is the key to a long and lasting time together. If you want your marriage to last, there is no room for quarreling, belittling, nagging, and strife. Joyful marriage has spousal respect and the understanding of each other's needs. Honor your spouse by avoiding strife. Your spouse should be your best friend for life.

Ephesians 4:29: *"Let no corrupting talk come out of your mouths, but only such as is good for building up, as it fits the occasion, that it may give grace to those that hear it."*

Being negative to your spouse is like holes in a ship's hull. Eventually, the ship will sink when the hull has acquired too many holes. On the other hand, positive reinforcing words build up your spouse. Using words such as "you are so smart," "so beautiful," "I'm blessed to be married to you," and "I Love You" are words that support and build up your spouse and strengthen your marriage.

Roman 14:19: *"So then let us pursue what makes for peace and for mutual up-building."*

Roman's verse addresses a very important issue, positive and negative communication. Are you a person who builds others up, or are you one that tears others down? Whether you are communicating with your spouse, children, neighbor, friend, or even someone that rubs you the wrong way, communicating with them in a positive up-building way is a Christian part of your strength.

I always try to treat others the way I would like to be treated. Show respect, humility, honor, and love the way Jesus did. If you remember this little habit, be a peacemaker, and you will feel better about yourself!

Ephesians 4:32: *"Be kind to one another, tenderhearted, forgiving one another, as God in Christ forgave you."*

Jesus's apostles were sinners, thieves, murderers, adulterers, liars, doubters, and even betrayed the Son of God, yet he forgave every one of them. Let Jesus be an example for us to be kind and forgiven. Carrying a grudge or spite in your heart only darkens your soul. Forgive the way Jesus has forgiven you.

Mathew 7:7: *"Ask and it will be given to you, seek, and you will find, knock, and it will be opened to you."*

Mathew 7:7 speaks to me and says that the power of prayer is the strength of our faith. Ask God with bold prayers, don't hold back. You may only get what you want sometimes, but you will be given what you need. This verse also tells me that a diligent and hard-working person will be rewarded. If it is a career that requires hours of work to get a head or a school diploma that you are working for, God has put you on this path to accomplish what is in your heart. Ask God for strength, and the door will be opened for you.

Psalms 139:13: *"You made all the delicate, inner parts of my body and knit me together in my mother's womb."*

The Bible says God knew you before you were created in your

mother's womb. God has a plan for all of us while we are walking this earth. Fulfill God's plan by diligently striving to be your best.

Proverbs 3:13: *"Blessed is the one who finds wisdom and the other one that gets understanding."*

Note that the Bible says "finds" wisdom. We have to work hard to become wise. Open your ears and listen to the truth, and act as a good Christian, and wisdom will find you.

Control, Wisdom, Respect, and Love:

Proverbs 20:3: *"It is an honor for a man to avoid strife, but every fool will be quarreling."*

It is easy to lose your temper in traffic or become upset when someone pulls in front of you and takes that parking space you have patiently been waiting for. In marriage, it takes a certain amount of personal restraint when quarreling with your spouse. Are you the spouse that digs up mistakes your partner made three years ago? Or are you bigger than that and resist the urge to dig up the past and not always be right or have your way?

I cannot emphasize this passage enough. Most marital arguments can be avoided if one partner takes the high road and lets the small misgivings fade away. Love your partner, understand their point of view, and move on. You may be right, but is it worth being the fool who argues just to get his point across?

Psalms 10:11: *"The mouth of the righteous is a fountain of life."*

Proverbs 15:1: *"The words of the reckless pierce like a sword, but the tongue of the wise brings healing."*

Proverbs 15:4: *"The soothing tongue is a tree of life, but a perverse tongue crushes the spirit."*

These three passages mean so much to me. Psalms 10:11 talks to me and says your words can bring joy to someone else. Have you recently said "I Love You" to your partner? Have you said, "I've been blessed to have you in my life" Words can heal, soothe and reinforce a marriage. Use healing and joyful words to strengthen your marriage. On the other hand, negative words can hurt and cut, eventually leaving your partner with wounds that may never heal. If you want a successful and happy marriage, use your words to build up your marriage and partner.

Mathew 19: 4-6: *"He answered, "Have you not read he who created them from the beginning made them male and female, and said, "Therefore a man shall leave his father and mother and hold fast to his wife, and the two shall become one flesh, so they are no longer two but one flesh. What therefore God has joined together let not man separate."*

Mathew 19 tells me that God has proclaimed husband and wife as a team. "A man should hold fast to his wife, and the two shall become one flesh...." In plain English, there is no 'I' in team. A husband has his wife's back, and a wife has her husband's back!

Galatians 5:26: *"Let us not become conceited, provoking one another, envying one another."*

When one spouse makes more money than the other, the successful spouse keeps reminding their partner of their greater contribution to the marriage. Or, a partner compares their relationship to other couples with larger houses, more expensive cars, or more expensive vacations. Such behavior can destroy the foundation of love and cause long-term damage. A rust on metal is just like envying a marriage. The metal will eventually corrode and fall apart and disintegrate into dust. A detailed discussion of marital conflicts is in Chapter 4.

Galatians 6:3: *"For if anyone thinks he is something when* *he is nothing, he deceives himself."*

As we grow older, we change. We become more valuable to our company. We may have our own company, and that business grows and becomes successful. Our success often inflates our egos, and our marriages begin to suffer. Stay the person your spouse married, and don't let your ego ruin your marriage.

1 Corinthians 13:11: *"When I was a child, I spoke like a child, I thought like a child, I reasoned like a child. When I became a man, I gave up childish ways."*

Marriage is one of the largest steps into adulthood. You are not responsible for just yourself but also for your spouse and, eventually, your family.

Romans 12:10: *"Love one another with brotherly affection. Outdo one another in showing honor."*

Your spouse is one of the greatest gifts our Heavenly Father has blessed us with. I like to think of this scripture in terms of a man. When most men (and some women) get their dream machine of a sports car, they treat that as the greatest thing ever. 'Pride of Ownership.' The same should hold for your spouse. We should treat our spouse as one of the greatest things to come into our lives with respect, honor, commitment, and unwavering love.

Strive To Be a Better Person:

Luke 6:37: *"Judge not, and you will not be judged."*

We did not marry our spouses to judge or be judged. Instead, honor and praise your spouse for keeping the marriage strong and binding with Love. Judging one another will deteriorate the Love and bonding in a marriage.

1 Thessalonians 5:16: *"Rejoice always, pray without ceasing,* *give thanks in all circumstances; for this is the will of God in Christ Jesus for you."*

In all circumstances, always love and give praise to God and the Son of God. When relationships are at their best, thank God for the happiness and joy you are experiencing. Pray for relationship healing and love when relationships hit a rocky and bumpy road.

Proverbs 12:22: *"Lying lips are an abomination to the Lord, but those who act faithfully are his delight."*

For a marriage to be built and survive, a foundation of truth is required. Be truthful to one another, and you will have a long and loving marriage.

1 Corinthians 16:14: *"Let all that you do be done in Love."*

God is the abundance of Love. Let us always follow in Jesus' footsteps and have Love in our hearts and towards one another, especially in a marriage.

Ephesians 4:32: *"Be kind and compassionate to one another, forgiving each other, just as Christ God forgave you."*

Learn from the examples and teaching Jesus did. We are all sinners, yet God, thru Jesus, has forgiven us and shown us compassion. In the same way, your spouse will never be perfect, yet we must learn compassion and forgiveness just in the same manner as Jesus did.

Ephesians 4:29: *"Do not let any unwholesome talk come out of your mouths, but only what is helpful for building others up according to their needs, that it may benefit those who listen."*

It hurts your spouse when you speak unwholesome talk about them... "My husband is such an imbecile.... My wife nags me all the time...." Instead, build your spouse up when talking to others... " My husband is awesome...... My wife is the greatest

103

wife ever...." Being positive and encouraging about your spouse is one of the greatest attributes you can have in a marriage.

Bring Jesus Closer to Your Heart:

1 John 3:18: *"Little children, let us love one another in action and truth, not in word or mouth."*

In today's society, the word 'Love' is thrown around so carelessly. I hear it on the radio when a famous singer tells his audience how he loves them or when you hear the word 'Love' on television or from a politician. Love is supposed to be backed up by action, as the bible professed. Love your spouse by helping with the chores of the house, sharing the child-rearing, and taking your share of all marital responsibilities.

Mathew 12:35: *"A good man brings good things out of the good stored up in him, and an evil man brings things out of the evil stored up in him. Blessed and enlighten others with your words."*

Kind and loving words help build up your spouse's character and self-esteem. Evil and reckless words cut like a knife, yet loving and caring words help nurture and strengthen the marriage.

Proverbs 18:13: *"He who answers a matter before he hears it.... It is folly and shame to him."*

Listen and understand your spouse's needs. Never assume what your spouse is thinking and needing. Your spouse may need a quiet moment alone in the evening because the children were hard to deal with, or your spouse had a very difficult and strenuous day in the office. Please don't assume your spouse is in a bad mood because of you. It may be an external event that they need to decompress from. Ask the right question, "How was your day?" or "Is there something I can do to help"? .... Then listen some more.

James 3:5: *"Likewise, the tongue is a small part of the body,* *but it makes great boasts... Consider what a great forest is set on fire by a small spark."*

A raging forest fire can only start with a small spark. Our tongue is sometimes our worst enemy. It can cut like a sword, ruin a marriage, and devastate a life. Be careful how you choose your words and actions.

Mathew 6:31: *"So do not worry, saying, 'What shall we eat?' 'What shall we drink?' For the pagans run after all these things, and your heavenly Father knows that you need."*

Always, 'Trust in God'.... During the good times, especially in the hard and very difficult times, God is there for you and knows what you need. If your marriage is in turmoil, faithful spouses turn to God for healing. Never give up on God; he will not give up on you.

James 4:8: *"Come near to God, and he will come near to you."*

It is tough for God to come into your house if your door is not open. It is even more difficult for God to enter a marriage if that door is shut. Spouses unite and pray for protection, growth, and Love in your marriage and family.

Ephesians 4:25: *"Therefore each of you must put off falsehood and speak truthfully to your neighbor, for we are all members of one body."*

Marriage is a team, or as the Bible points out, marriage is one body. Be truthful to each other for the sake of your marriage.

Romans 14:19: *"So then let us 'pursue' what makes for peace and for mutual upbuilding."*

The goal of a marriage is to grow strong every day. Days turn to years, and years turn into decades. The only way for a marriage to grow and strengthen is to pursue peace, harmony, and Love with each other, with Jesus in the middle.

Galatians 5:13: *"For you were called to freedom, brothers. Only do not use your freedom as an opportunity for the flesh, but through love, serve one another."*

With the lust and pornography in our media and the world around us, we can become entangled in the flesh. Never stop loving your spouse, and pray that the chains of the flesh never bind you. Bible tells us to run from temptation and never believe that we alone can stand the test, but on the other hand, turn your back on the dark side and pray for strength. God will always have an escape route waiting for you!

Ephesians 4: 1-3: *"I therefore, a prisoner for the Lord, urge you to walk in a manner worthy of the calling to which you have been called, 2. With all humility and gentleness, with patience, bearing with one another love, 3. Eager to maintain the unity of the Spirit in the bond of peace."*

Healthy Christian marriages walk as prisoners of the Lord seeking the Lord's guidance, grace, humility, and Love. Spouses should always be gentle and patient with each other and maintain God's Spirit in their marriage.

Proverbs 25:11: *"A word filthy spoken is like apples of gold in a setting of silver."*

Healthy communication is vital for relationships. Scholars tell us that the meaning of this verse is a representation of good compared to the "Golden Apple set in Silver." Speaking encouraging and positive communication is golden to the ears of the receiver.

1 Corinthians 13: 14-5: *"Love is patient, love is kind. It does not envy, it does not boast, it is not proud. It does not dishonor* *others, it is not self-seeking, it is not easily angered, it keeps no record of wrongs."*

Love is mentioned 759 times in the Bible (NLT). The foundation of everything being good, kind, and generous is based on Love. If you have Love in your heart, you will not judge others, you will be kind, you are an even-tempered person, and you have forgiveness in your heart. Love conquers all.

Philippians 2:3: *"Do nothing from rivalry or conceit, but in humility count others more significant than yourselves."*

Place others before you. Jesus said, "Our time on earth is just like the morning mist." How

do you want to spend your time? Your very short time on this earth? Do you want to live conceited and just for your self-gratification, or do you choose to help others?

2 Corinthians 8:21: *"For we are taking pains to do what is right, not only in the eyes of the Lord but also in the eyes of man."*

Walking the narrow path the Lord has set in front of us takes work. Straying from the Lord's path and seeking our own way would be much easier. Jesus is watching our every step, and so are the people around us. Be an inspiration and a good example to others.

Luke 9:23: *"If any of you want to be my followers, you must forget about yourself. You must take up your cross every day and follow me."*

Jesus teaches us to leave our past lives behind us and live our new Christian lives in faith and obedience. Paul says it the best, "I die daily," meaning every day Paul did not know what the day would bring, persecution, stoning, harassment, and even execution. Live the life Jesus lived by Love and honor.

1 Corinthians 15 20-28: *"But Christ has indeed been raised from the dead, the first fruits of those who have fallen asleep. 21 For since death came through a man, the resurrection of the dead comes also through a man. 22 For as in Adam all die, so in Christ all will be made alive. 23 But each in turn: Christ, the first fruits; then when he comes, those who belong to him. 24 Then the end will come when he hands over the kingdom to God the Father after he has destroyed all dominion, authority, and power. 25 For he must reign until he has put all his enemies under his feet. 26. The last enemy to be destroyed is death. 27 For he "has put everything under his feet." Now when it says "everything" has been put under him, it is clear that this does not include God himself, who put everything under Christ. 28 When he has done this, then the Son himself will be made subject to him who put everything under Him so that God may be all in all."*

Paul argues in 1 Corinthians 15 that if there was no resurrection of Jesus, then there is no church, and most importantly, our sins would not be forgiven. For death began with Adam, Life begins with Christ.

2 Timothy 1:7: *"For God gave us a spirit not to fear but of power, love, and self-control."*

This verse is so powerful and enlightening. God gave us all a spirit, a spirit to triumph, a spirit for self-control, a spirit of power over our actions, and a spirit of Love. Develop your spirits so you can become the best Christian you can be. We have a choice. Ask God for direction and for the Holy Spirit to come into life.

Ephesians 4:29: *"Let no corrupting talk come out of your mouths, but only such as good for building up, as it fits the occasion, that it may give grace to those who hear it."*

The tongue can be a sharpened sword. It can cut deep and leave painful and emotional scars. Choose your words to build and honor others.

Marriage and Family:

Mark 3:25: *"A home filled with strife and division destroys itself."*

This verse should be the first sentence in every marriage handbook. Team marriage cannot withstand strife, division, ill-respect, dishonesty, and turmoil. As Jesus tells us, "A house foundation built on sand will not withstand time." Build your marriage on a rock-solid foundation by loving, honoring, respecting, and communicating.

Proverbs 21:19: *"It is better to live in a desert land than with a quarrelsome and fretful woman."*

Waking up to a nagging and quarrelsome spouse would be like living with an infected tooth. (My analogy) Wouldn't you want to grow old with a spouse that would rather Love, respect, and be a joy as a partner or a spouse that argues and nags?

John 8:7: *"And as they continue to ask him, he stood up and said to them, "Let him who is without sin among you be the first to throw a stone at her."*

We are all sinners… Jesus called us out and asked if anyone around us was without sin. Understanding that we are all sinners, we must forgo judging and accepting others with Love and understanding.

Proverbs 18-22: *"He who finds a wife finds a good thing and obtains favor from the Lord."*

I have been so blessed to have found Claudette and called her my wife. Having Claudette as my marriage partner shows me that the living God loves us and cares for our needs.

James 3:14-15: *"But if you have bitter jealousy and selfish ambition in your hearts, do not boast and be false to the truth. This is not the wisdom that comes down from above, but is earthly, unspiritual, demonic."*

You have heard the expression, "Be careful about what you wish for." God has a plan for us, yet God gives us the right to make our own choices. Make sure your decision is in line with God's plan. Pray, meditate, and listen to the quiet voice in your head; God is speaking to you.

Revelation 21:8: *"But as for the cowardly, the faithless, the detestable, as for murderers, the sexually immoral, sorcerers, idolaters, and all liars, their portion will be in the lake that burns with fire and sulfur, which is the second death."*

1 John 2:4: *"Whoever says, "I know him" but does not keep his commandments is a liar, and the truth is not in him."*

1 Peter 3:7: *"Likewise, husbands, live with your wives in an understanding way, showing honor to the women as the weaker vessel, since they are heirs with you of the grace of life, so that your prayers may not be hindered."*

Ephesians 5:33: *"However, let each one of you love his wife as himself, and let the wife see that she respects her husband."*

These four biblical verses, Revelations 21:8, 1 John 2:4, 1 Peter 3:7, and Ephesians 5:33, teach us to honor, respect, and Love our spouse. There will be consequences for those spouses that are cheaters, liars, abusers, and those that dishonor the covenant of marriage.

Proverbs 3:15: *"The righteous hates falsehood, but the wicked brings shame and disgrace."*

Wisdom is greater than any materialistic possessions. A believer in Christ enjoys fellowship with God and relies on his faith in God to provide for him. On the other hand, a person who does not believe in Jesus and cherishes earthly possessions will miss eternal life.

Mathew 5:9: ESV: *"Blessed are the peacemakers, for they shall be called sons of God."*

Be the peacemaker in your family.... Avoid strife, criticism, nagging, and judging your spouse. Sometimes, we need to take the high road, turn the other cheek, and be the Christian in the room.

John 16:33: ESV: *"I have said these things to you, that in me you may have peace. In the world, you will have tribulation. But take heart; I have overcome the world."*

It will rain on everyone, Christian and Non-Christian. There is refuge in Jesus. Allow the Holy Spirit to comfort you with eternal peace.

Proverbs 1:7: ESV: *"The fear of the Lord is the beginning of knowledge; fools despise wisdom and instruction."*

And

Proverbs 18:15: ESV: *"An intelligent heart acquires knowledge, and the ear of the wise seeks knowledge."*

And

Proverbs 9:9: ESV: *"Give instruction to a wise man, and he will be still wiser, teach a righteous man, and he will increase in learning."*

All four scriptures (John 16, Proverbs 1, Proverbs 18, and Proverbs 9) enlighten us to honor Jesus for his teachings and sacrifice for our eternal existence.

Christians should refrain from taking knowledge to outweigh the Lord in priority and the Holy Spirit's teaching.

Allow the Holy Spirit to teach you growth and knowledge to strengthen your marriage.

Luke 11: 9-10: *"So I say to you, ask, and it will be given to you; seek, and you will find; knock, and it will be opened to you. For everyone who asks, receives; and he who seeks, finds; and to him who knocks, it will be opened."*

Do not give up…. Keep being persistent in whatever you do. This passage comes directly from the Lord's Prayer. Pray with confidence as God hears all your prayers.

Marriage is one of God's special gifts to us. If your marriage is experiencing turmoil, pray with conviction and watch the Lord take charge.

1 Peter 3:7: ESV: *"In the same way, you husbands must give honor to your wives. Treat your wife with understanding as you live together."*

Husbands have the responsibility to treat and honor their wives with respect and dignity. Living together as equals and understanding that you are a team inundated with life's turmoil. Marriages require team harmony to fight off Satan's attacks.

Ephesians 4:2-3: *"With all humility and gentleness, with patience, bearing with one another in love, eager to maintain the unity of the Spirit in the bond of peace."*

> Ephesians 4 tells us the five ways people obtain unity with the Spirit.
> 1. Live in humility
> 2. Have a gentle heart
> 3. Be patient
> 4. Show Love and Kindness in everything you do
> 5. Seek God and the word of Jesus.

A strong and successful marriage contains all five of Ephesian's teachings.

1 Peter 3:1-2: *"Likewise, wives, be subject to your own husbands, so that even if some do not obey the word, they may be won without a word by the conduct of their wives, when they see your respectful and pure conduct."*

Actions speak louder than words. Wives, stay strong in your faith even if your husbands are not believers in Christ. With your faithful actions, the Holy Spirit can do tremendous work.

Ephesians 4:2-3: *"With all humility and gentleness, with patience, bearing with one another in love, eager to maintain the unity of the Spirit in the bond of peace."*

Humility, kindness, gentleness, patience, and Love are the bonds every successful marriage contains.

1 John 5:18: NSV: *"We know that everyone who has been born of God does not keep on sinning, but he who was born of God protects him, and the evil one does not touch him."*

I love how John starts with "We ."I take away that Christian marriages are a 'Big We .'"We, as a Christian team, will work through our differences." "We are in this marriage to the end, "For God is before us, who dare be against us."

If you are struggling with your marriage, get on your knees and pray for God's protection and that Satan will not break your marriage covenant.

Proverbs 22:6: ESV: *"Train up a child in the way he should go; even when he is old, he will not depart from it."*

The greatest gift you can give your children is the gift of the Spirit and the teaching of Jesus Christ. Children are the most precious gift parents could ever receive from God.

With this gift, a parent must keep their children from the allure of evil.

Our mission on this earth is to teach, train, and lead by example what is appropriate behavior, and also, our children must learn that there are consequences for behavior (Good and Bad). Help your children begin their life's journey with God-given direction.

I always tell young parents that we fill our children's toolboxes with Godly direction, values, morals, strong character, and Love. When our children grow up to be adults, they can pull those tools and use what we placed in the toolbox for them.

Pray that our children never stray to the dark side and stay on God's path. From the very beginning, God gave Adam and Eve a choice. Pray that our children always make the right choice, and sometimes they will not make the best decision; that is why we as parents are there to catch and Love them.

Love them Unconditionally:

Ecclesiastes 3:1-8: ESV: *"For everything, there is a season and a time for every matter under heaven; a time to be born, and a time to die, a time to plant, and a time to pluck up what is planted; a time to kill, and a time to heal; a time to break down, and a time to build up; a time to weep, and a time to laugh; a time to mourn, and a time to dance; a time to cast away stones, and a time to gather stones together; a time to embrace, and a time to refrain from embracing."*

God controls the universe, physics, science, and even our lives. We are the miracle works of our Heavenly Father, who loves us more than imaginable.

Ecclesiastes teaches us that our life will always have changes. Nothing is consistent, it will rain on everyone, and the sun will shine on all. Our faith will triumph because our hearts and soul trust the Lord whatever comes our way, good and bad.

Job in the Bible was a prosperous, healthy man with a wonderful life and family. God permitted Satan to ruin his life literally. Job lost his possessions, children, and health, but in the end, Job refused to curse God even when his wife told him to curse God and roll over and die. Job's faith and Love for God are an inspiration to all Christians. In the end, God restored and rewarded Job for his unwavering faith.

2 Timothy 3:16-17: *"All Scripture is breathed out by God and profitable for teaching, for reproof, for correction, and for training in righteousness, that the man of God may be competent, equipped for every good work."*

In Second Timothy, the Bible scripture tells us that God breathes the verses onto the holy pages thru the writers. The Bible is not a person's figment of their imagination but a living document that God almighty has instilled his road map for us to follow for salvation and to equip us for our journey through life on earth.

Don't let time go by and not share the joy that you have acquired. In Colossians 4:5-6, St. Paul writes that we must share the joy that Jesus Christ has given us. We have something others long for, even secretly desire, yet it evades them. What is that? Knowing Jesus and the love he shows us is the joy in our hearts.

John 15:1-27: *"I am the true vine, and my Father is the vinedresser. Every branch in me that does not bear fruit he takes away, and every branch that does bear fruit he prunes that it may bear more fruit. Already you are clean because of the word that I have spoken to you. Abide in me, and I in you. As the branch cannot bear fruit by itself unless it abides in the vine, neither can you unless you abide in me. I am the vine; you are the branches. Whoever abides in me and I in him, he it is that bears much fruit,* *for apart from me, you can do nothing."*

Jesus explains to us that he is the "True Vine" and "My Father (God) is the vinedresser." Knowing and understanding that the Son of God is Jesus, we progress from mortal oblivion to Spiritual Salvation. ("Bear Fruit"). Jesus says, "As the branch cannot bear fruit by itself unless it abides in the vine." Meaning our salvation, we cannot do it alone, but we are only saved thru Jesus ("The vine").

Write down your favorite scriptures

What do the scripture(s) mean to you?

Acknowledgement / References:

Bradley R.E. Wright, (2010), Christians Are Hate-Filled Hypocrites ...and Other Lies You've Been Told, (Minneapolis, MN: Bethany House, s

W. Bradford Wilcox and Elizabeth Williamson, (2007), "The Cultural Contradictions of Mainline Family Ideology and Practice," in American Religions and the Family, edited by Don S. Browning and David A. Clairmont (New York: Columbia University Press.

The American Journal of Family Therapy: Romantic Physical Affection Types and Relationship Satisfaction

Journal of Happiness Studies: How's Life at Home? New Evidence on Marriage and the Set Point for Happiness of Christian Families.

Research: Personality and Individual Differences: Christian Partner Depressions, Christian Partner Dating, Courtship, and Attractions.

Indiana University Bloomington: The two-month curse: don't let January workout resolutions fade for Christian marriages.

J Consult Clinic Psychol. : Benefits of recruiting participants with friends and increasing social support for weight loss and maintenance.

Marriage.com: 11 Ways to Have a Quality Time With Your Partner

J Marriage Fam. : Time for Each Other: Work and Family Constraints Among Couples

W. Bradford Wilcox & Jeffrey Dew: The Date Night Opportunity

Marriage.com: 10 Benefits of Physical Intimacy in Your Relationship

30 Virtues of a Christian Marriage, By Sylvia Smith, July 27, 2020

In Marriage as in Life, Weak Is Strong, Dave Harvey, May 11, 2020

Fight for your marriage – even if everyone tells you not to. New Spring Church

W. Bradford Wilcox & Jeffrey Dew: The Date Night Opportunity

Marriage.com: 10 Benefits of Physical Intimacy in Your Relationship

World War Two pictures: Ownership: Gary Cunitz

Institute for Family Studies, March 4th, 2020, By Brian Hollar

Internet search:

The following resources were helpful:

General Christian Marriage Statistics and Information

Christian marriages

Christian divorces

statistics on black vs. white Christian marriages and divorces.

Christian marriage statistics for ages 25-54

General Social Christian Marriage Survey 1972 – 2018, Two racial segments of the United States: Marriage of White Population and Black Population

Brian Hollar Institute for Family Studies, March 4th, 2020.

Dr. Goldberg, The New Female and Male Relationship, William Morrow & Co.

First edition (Jan 1, 1981).

Biblical references

Google references, New International Bible (NIV), Wikipedia, Bible Cross References, Christian Bible reference site, Bible Study Tools.

All scripture quotations, unless otherwise indicated, are taken from the New International Version (NIV), copyright © 1973, 1975, 1977, 1998, 2000 by Biblica, Inc.™.

Please note that all websites listed herein were accurate at the time of publication but may change in the future or cease to exist. Listing website references and resources does not imply endorsement of the site's contents. Groups, corporations, ownership, and organizations are listed for informational purposes only. Listing references and resources does not imply endorsement of their activities by the publisher or author.

www.ingramcontent.com/pod-product-compliance
Lightning Source LLC
Chambersburg PA
CBHW051532120626
46551CB00012B/1193